Professional Ethics

Professional Ethics

A Trust-Based Approach

Terrence M. Kelly

LEXINGTON BOOKS
Lanham • Boulder • New York • London

Published by The Rowman & Littlefield Publishing Group, Inc.
An imprint of The Rowman & Littlefield Publishing Group, Inc.
4501 Forbes Boulevard, Suite 200, Lanham, Maryland 20706
www.rowman.com

Unit A, Whitacre Mews, 26-34 Stannary Street, London SE11 4AB

British Library Cataloguing in Publication Information Available

Library of Congress Cataloging-in-Publication Data

Names: Kelly, Terrence M., author.
Title: Professional ethics : a trust-based approach / Terrence M. Kelly.
Description: Lanham : Lexington Books, 2018. | Includes bibliographical references and index.
LCCN 2017061423 (print) | LCCN 2017059287 (ebook) | ISBN 9781498513630 (Electronic) | ISBN 9781498513623 (cloth : alk. paper) | ISBN 9781498513647 (pbk. : alk. paper)
Subjects: LCSH: Professional ethics.
Classification: : LCC BJ1725 (print) | LCC BJ1725 .K45 2018 (ebook) | DDC 174--dc23
LC record available at https://lccn.loc.gov/2017061423

∞™ The paper used in this publication meets the minimum requirements of American National Standard for Information Sciences Permanence of Paper for Printed Library Materials, ANSI/NISO Z39.48-1992.

Printed in the United States of America

For Elias and all other future trustworthy professionals.
May they make the world a better place.

Contents

Acknowledgments

Successful professional practice is made possible by the existence of supportive communities, and so it is with this book, which owes its existence to the contributions of many members of my professional and personal community.

First and foremost I would like to thank my two Cheryl Mandalas— one my wife and the "other" Cheryl my mother-in-law. Cheryl-the-wife offered unstinting support, enlightening conversation, and editorial skill during the trials and travails of writing this book. Cheryl-the-elder served as my master editor and selflessly poured over the entire text, more than once and often on short notice, and offered endlessly valuable corrections, thoughts, and ideas. Without the two Cheryls, the book simply would not exist.

I would also like to thank Jana Hodges-Kluck at Lexington Books for her encouragement and support during the writing and production of the book.

The book benefited from audience feedback and conversations at meetings of the Association for Practical and Professional Ethics, the American Society for Bioethics and the Humanities, and the American Philosophical Association.

The book also benefited from comments by an anonymous reviewer for Lexington Books, and by anonymous reviewers of an earlier essay on conflict of interest for the *Cambridge Quarterly for Healthcare Ethics*. I would like to thank my professional ethics students at the University of Alaska Anchorage (UAA) who offered important and helpful feedback on earlier drafts of the book. My colleagues in the philosophy department and Alaska Ethics Center at UAA also provided important ideas and feedback for the book.

The book project was supported by travel grants and course releases from the College of Arts and Sciences at UAA, and I thank Dean John Stalvey for his support of the project.

Last but not least I want to thank James Lord, Alisa Carroll, Danielle Dittmer, and all the other professionals who have served as personal exemplars of "the trustworthy professional," and who provided instrumental support during the writing of this book. Finally thanks to my mentor, James Bohman, who guided me into professional philosophy and continues to serve as an inspiration.

Elements of chapter 6 appeared in "Conflicts About Conflict of Interest: A Comparison of "Performance" and "Trustworthiness" Models of COI in the Context of Industry Relations with Physicians," *Cambridge Quarterly of Healthcare Ethics* 25, no. 3 (2016): 526–535. Reprinted with permission.

Introduction

The professions stand at an important crossroads. Beset by scandal, changing social expectations, and economic pressures, the credibility and legitimacy of the professions have been subject to unprecedented scrutiny. Some critics argue that the idea of a profession—understood as a self-governing expert community committed to a service ideal—is a sham that simply promotes the economic interests of professionals. On this view, the professions are but cartels, aimed at monopolizing markets and promoting the bottom line of professional enterprises. Others argue that professionals are no longer worthy of the unique trust extended to them because professional misconduct is so ubiquitous that the idea of entrusting critical interests to professionals is no longer rational. Aside from misconduct, changing social expectations have made the idea of trusting professionals obsolete. In medicine, for instance, the paternalistic idea of "doctor knows best" has been subject to fatal moral and legal critique. Even virtuous doctors cannot help but introduce values into their medical decisions—values they have no right to impose on patients. Finally, even some professionals themselves suggest that professional practice would be more lucrative without the rigorous moral demands created by professionalization.

Is the idea of professionalism obsolete—a dangerous dinosaur of the past that promotes inefficiency and exposes the public to the unscrupulous? The central thesis of this book is that the rumors of the death of professionalism have been greatly exaggerated. The idea that some occupational groups should be organized into relatively self-governing communities committed to strict ethical standards in the promotion of a service ideal is a necessary consequence of the fact that some occupations, by their very nature, offer their expert assistance to others in a way that requires reliance under conditions of knowledge and power asymmetry. When people rely on doctors, lawyers, bankers, engineers, accountants, therapists, and the like, they must *entrust* important interests to the discretionary care of the professional. This is a functional imperative of the professions. If clients, patients, students, and the public were not willing to extend their trust to professionals, many of those occupations would not exist, while others would be but empty shells of what they are currently.

This book explores the role of trust in understanding the logic of the professions, particularly the unique ethical demands placed on professionals and professional communities. Chapter 1 explores the apparent divergence between ordinary morality and professional ethics. Why should professionals be held to unusually strict standards of conduct? Some have argued it is because they have promised to do so. But this does not explain *why* they should promise to do so. Others point to the important role of professionals in satisfying social needs. However, these approaches do not explain why professionals have obligations to the specific clients, patients, and students they serve. A "third way" is offered by considering professional obligations in light of the trust that professionals must invite and develop given the defining goal, or *telos,* of the practice.

Chapter 2 explores the instrumental, ethical, and moral reasons professionals have to invite and develop the trust of would-be clients, patients, and the general public. Instrumentally, trust is necessary if professionals are to achieve the goals of their practice and do well as economic agents. For instance, patients who do not trust doctors avoid them—this is bad for their health *and* for the practice of medicine. Ethically, the promotion of a trusting relationship with clients and patients offers a way for professionals to flourish in light of the valuable goods promoted by professional practice: health, justice, safety, financial security, and efficiency. This creates a framework for professional virtue and a means by which professionals form ethical communities. Morally, the formation of trusting "I-Thou" relationships is necessary if professionals are to be responsive to their moral accountability to those they serve. Professionals also typically benefit from the social scheme that creates and promotes the professionals as self-governing and monopolizing communities. Professionals have an obligation as a matter of "fair play" to honor their end of this social bargain and, among other things, develop the trust that is necessary to perform their practice well.

Professionals have good reasons to develop trust in those they serve, but the unique nature of the client-professional relationship makes this challenging. Professionals operate in relatively anonymous conditions in which there are stark knowledge and power asymmetries between themselves and those they typically serve. Can trust in professionals be rational? It can, provided that professionals are *effectively trustworthy.* Professionals are so when they can be relied upon to responsibly care for the interests entrusted to them *and* are able to effectively communicate that trustworthiness to others. Chapter 3 explores what it means for professionals to be trustworthy. Here the literature can be divided into two schools of thought. "Instrumental" trustworthiness is created through a harmony of interests between trustor and trustee. A trustee is worthy of trust only when it is in his or her interests to be reliable (as in certain economic arrangements). "Dispositional" trustworthiness, on the other hand, is defined as the possession of certain virtues, such as conscientiousness, by which the trustee is reliable, even when being so is not in his or her interests. Because instrumental and dispositional trustworthiness each are limited, professional trustworthiness is best understood in terms of both interests and virtues. Instrumental trustworthiness is created by institutional arrangements and disciplinary systems that dis-incentivize misconduct. Dispositional trustworthiness is created when professionals have the kind of character dispositions by which they are responsive to the needs of those they serve. Virtues such as integrity, loyalty, beneficence, respect for autonomy, honesty, discretion, diligence, and resilience are trust-warranting properties, the possession of which make professionals trustworthy.

Individual professionals alone cannot accomplish the development of trustworthiness. Instrumental trustworthiness requires institutional arrangements, and dispositional trustworthiness requires professional education and socialization. For these reasons, professional trustworthiness requires the work of the professional community as an *ethical community*. Chapter 4 explores the way in which professional communities support an ongoing ethical discourse oriented toward interpreting the community telos and identifying the ethical standards of the profession. The outcomes of such discourses are concretized in oaths, codes of ethics, professional self-understandings, standards of training and education, and appropriate disciplinary schemes. Importantly, dispositional trustworthiness cannot be achieved through a "compliance paradigm," by which ethical conduct is tantamount to following compulsory rules. Professional communities do better when adopting an "authenticity paradigm," in which the self-understanding of the professional is efficaciously linked with the professional virtues.

Internally, the profession-as-ethical-community works to develop trustworthy professionals. However, trust is threatened both by "bad character and poor information."[1] Chapter 5 explores the ways that professionals and professional communities work externally to communicate professional trustworthiness to those they intend to serve. Professional communities work to communicate the trustworthiness of practitioners by constructing and maintaining a professional *reputation*. Professional reputations prime public expectations regarding the trustworthiness of professional role-players. However, reputation alone is not enough. Individual practitioners themselves must be able to effectively signal their identity as bona fide members of the profession, as well as their own personal trustworthiness. Only when they possess trust-warranting properties and are adept at signaling it are professionals effectively trustworthy.

The variety of signals offered by professionals are assurances made to clients, patients, or the general public with the aim of inducing trust. For some ethicists, assurances aimed at inviting trust are essentially promises even if they do not follow the specific linguistic promising convention. By inviting trust through the symbolic presentation of the professional self, professionals make an *implied promise* that they are responsive to the needs of those they serve and can be counted on to responsibly care for them.

Given the good reasons professionals have to be effectively trustworthy, chapter 6 explores the reasons for finding conflicts of interest blameworthy. Professionals operate under such a conflict when they practice in arrangements, as viewed by a reasonable observer, that would significantly tempt a professional of normal psychology to place his or her own interests above the interests of those they serve. Conflicts of interest are toxic to trust because they make professionals less trustworthy and undermine the effective communication of one's trustworthiness. Moreover, when professionals practice with avoidable conflicts of interest, they are rightly held blameworthy for failing to take seriously the risks to their integrity created by such conflicts, and the signal they send to trust-evaluators as to their trustworthiness. While some professionals argue that conflicts of interest are only blameworthy when it can be demonstrated that professional integrity has been compromised, such "compromised performance" approaches are unsatisfactory because they fail to honor the professional duty to be effectively trustworthy. Moreover, such an approach to conflicts of interest fails to adequately protect the public since the conflict is only held blameworthy *after* the conflict has created negative outcomes for patients and clients. Conflicts are better assessed instead through *ex ante* evaluation of the professional's effective trustworthiness. Although unavoidable conflicts are not blameworthy, they are still toxic to trust and must be carefully disclosed and managed.

Finally, while professionals have good reasons to invite, develop, and honor the trust of those they serve, there are ethical limitations as to the range of trust that professionals should invite and honor. In chapter 7, it is argued that professionals are not simply agents who are but mere instruments of the client's will. Professionals are trustworthy when they are fiduciaries committed to high ethical standards developed in light of the trust appropriate given the professional telos. For this reason, trustworthy professionals exercise professional moral agency and must consider requests from clients and patients in light of the promises they and their profession make when inviting trust from those they intend to serve. For instance, if a patient asks for a prescription of unnecessary or excessive opioids, the physician must refuse to honor this kind of trust. Such trust is uninvited and inappropriate given the purpose of medicine.

Refusal of service is much more controversial when it is based on the professional's *personal* moral agency. Some ethicists argue that as a matter of moral integrity professionals should be able to refuse service that, while legal and legitimate from a professional standpoint, is immoral by the lights of the professional's personal conscience. Such arguments go too far and would allow professionals to impose their personal values on the public—an outcome contrary to the professional's role of providing effective expert assistance. However, under certain circumstances, conscientious objection to particular practices can be accommodated provided that it is reasonable, non-discriminatory, and does not burden patients and clients.

Whistleblowing also represents a fundamental limit of professional trust. While professionals invite informational trust from clients and employers, that invitation must be understood in light of professional moral agency. Under certain circumstances, professionals have a duty to set aside their loyalty and confidentiality, and disclose the wrongdoings of employers and clients. The damage of whistleblowing (for both professional and employer/client) can be minimized by the creation of a transparent and decentered communicative culture that encourages disclosure of "bad news" as a valued part of the organization. In such a context, whistleblowing moves from being an act of disloyalty to an act of loyalty. Such communicative cultures bolster trust generally in organizations, which is associated with a variety of positive business outcomes.

The aim of this book is largely reconstructive. It takes the implicit logic of the professional practice and idealizes it into a realistic utopianism.[2] As a reconstruction, the ideals advanced are aspirations worth pursuing in their own right, but they are aspirations that many professionals and professional communities already pursue, however imperfectly.

Despite the scandals and changing expectations, there are still many trustworthy professionals out there—indeed most professionals are relatively trustworthy practitioners. This is good news for the public because relying on, and making oneself vulnerable to, the discretion of professionals is the only way to satisfy many of the most important human needs in modern societies. When clients, students, patients, and the general public trust professionals, they demand responsible care of their vulnerability. Virtuous professionals take up that demand as their calling.

NOTES

1. Michael Bacharach and Diego Gambetta, "Trust in Signs," in *Trust and Society*, ed. Karen Cook (New York: Russell Sage Foundation, 2001): 150.

2. John Rawls, *Justice as Fairness: A Restatement*, ed. Erin Kelly (Cambridge, MA: Belknap Press, 2001): 4.

Chapter One

A Puzzle About Professional Ethics

On June 8th, 1998 Colorado prosecutor Mark Pautler faced an extraordinary ethical dilemma. William Neal, a sadistic killer, had killed three people—in one case by splitting open the victim's skull with a maul—and kidnapped three others. Neal then left the kidnapping victims in an apartment, instructing them to have police contact him when they arrived. Deputy Sheriff Sheryl Zimmerman contacted Neal by phone and began a long conversation with him during which he confessed to (or rather bragged about) the three murders as well as the kidnappings. He also talked about surrendering to authorities. Before doing so, he wanted a lawyer.

Unsurprisingly, this was not Neal's first brush with the law. He had worked previously with a defense lawyer named Daniel Platter, with whom he now requested to speak before surrendering. Efforts to reach Plattner failed, however, because his phone number was disconnected. Prosecutor Pautler, who was at the scene, believed Platter had left the practice of law. When Zimmerman told Neal of this development Neal asked to speak to a public defender instead, and Zimmerman agreed to contact one.

For various reasons, Zimmerman did not do so. Zimmerman and the other police present were concerned that a public defender would advise Neal to stop speaking with authorities, which would have prevented his apprehension. At this point, Pautler, the prosecutor, decided to pose as a public defender. Zimmerman told Neal that a public defender named "Mark Palmer" had arrived at the scene. Zimmerman then pretended to brief "Palmer" on the situation before handing him the phone. Neal was completely fooled by the ruse and took "Palmer" to be a public defender who was his legal counsel. One of his requests for turning himself in was that "his lawyer" would be present when he was taken into custody. "Palmer," actually Pautler, responded that he would be there. Neal then divulged his location and was peacefully taken into custody. Neal would later be convicted and sentenced to death for his killing spree.

Along with the good work of Sheriff Zimmerman, Pautler's deception of Neal was the key in the apprehension of this dangerous and deranged criminal. Neal had bragged that he had killed over 500 people, and that he would kill more if provoked. His peaceful apprehension made the public safer. Mark Pautler's reward for his savvy actions? The state bar filed disciplinary charges against him, and his license to practice law was suspended. [1]

"ORDINARY" MORALITY AND PROFESSIONAL ROLE OBLIGATIONS

The Paulter case highlights a puzzle about professional ethics. Professionals seem to have obligations that are quite different from those of "ordinary morality." Except perhaps for the strict Kantian, Pautler's actions would likely be justifiable from the standpoint of general morality. After all, he helped apprehend a murderer who posed a genuine threat to the public. Yet, because he was a lawyer, Pautler's deception was far from heroic and, at least as far as the Colorado State Bar was concerned, warranted professional discipline. While the Pautler case is unusually dramatic, the tension between ordinary morality and professional ethics is not.

There are a variety of ways in which professional role obligations seem different from the obligations that emerge in ordinary life. In some cases, professional role obligations are similar in kind, but different in degree, from ordinary obligations. For example, it is widely recognized that professionals have obligations to honesty and confidentiality that are far stricter than those in ordinary morality. In everyday life, there is a prima facie obligation to be honest, but there are also a wide variety of cases in which deception is justifiable. In the professions, on the other hand, the range of justifiable deception is exceptionally narrow. Even in medicine, where paternalistic deception was long and widely tolerated, if not encouraged, deception of patients is now prohibited except in the most extreme cases. This is also true in terms of confidentiality where doctors, lawyers, engineers, and teachers have obligations of discretion regarding sensitive client information that goes far beyond what is typically expected.

While some professional role obligations are different in degree from ordinary morality, others seem different in *kind*. Consider romantic relationships. It is generally permissible for consenting adults to develop and maintain romantic relationships. Indeed, one might say that consenting adults have a *right* to develop and maintain such relationships if they so choose. However, for professionals such as lawyers, teachers, social workers, and therapists even consensual romantic relationships with their patients, clients or students are prohibited.

Prohibitions on romantic relationships seem to fall in the category of professional obligations that Bernard Geert refers to as "precautionary" obligations.[2] Precautionary obligations prohibit or restrict particular actions that might not be inherently wrong, but are forbidden nonetheless because of the inappropriate appearance they create, or because they contribute to a culture in which wrongdoing is otherwise encouraged. In the legal profession, judges and prosecutors are typically required to avoid even the "appearance" of a conflict of interest, even though the mere appearance of such conflicts would not create bias or prejudice. For instance, United States federal judicial ethics rules forbid judges (and their law clerks) from owning even a single share of stock in corporations directly involved in their cases.[3] While it seems unlikely that owning a single share of a corporation would bias a judge, the appearance of impropriety alone is enough, it is argued, to justify such prohibitions.

SEPARATISM IN PROFESSIONAL ETHICS

How is the tension between ordinary morality and professional role morality to be explained? One radical approach would be to hold that professional role obligations are not derived from morality at all, but are justified relative to a separate source of obligation. From this perspective, professional role obligations are not only distinct from ordinary morality; they can require *violations* of ordinary morality. As Benjamin Freedman provocatively puts it, professional role obligations sometimes require professionals to "do evil."[4] Such a position, dubbed "radical separatism" by some commentators[5] is attractive in that it takes seriously the distinctive and puzzling nature of professional obligations. One could argue that Mark Pautler, for instance, was perfectly justified in his deception from a moral point of view, but because legal ethics are derived from a nonmoral source, he nonetheless violated his obligations as a lawyer.

While attractive, such a position is unsatisfactory for a number of reasons. As a descriptive matter, it is not clear that professionals actually have obligations to "do evil." Certainly, uncontroversial cases are hard to come by. Freedman cites cases such as physicians observing confidentiality even the face of court proceedings, but only the most flatfooted utilitarian would consider such a case as a clear obligation to do evil. As Alan Gewirth points out, arguments for radical separatism tend to conflate "morality," understood roughly as what we owe one another as free and equal persons, with "ordinary morality," which consists of what persons owe one another in everyday, noninstitutionalized settings.[6] Refusing to divulge information in a court proceeding might be a violation of one's obligations as an ordinary person.

However, it does not follow that doing so is always immoral. Unique circumstances may, and often do, create unique *moral* obligations.

The descriptive weakness of strong separatism highlights a number of conceptual problems. Radical separatists must assume that no satisfactory answer can be provided to explain the unique nature of professional role obligations from the perspective of morality itself. However, severing the link between professional role obligations and morality altogether raises the thorny question of how professional role obligations gain their normative force if not from morality. A common answer is to point to the unique features of the *role* and argue that it is the role, and not morality, that explains the normativity of the professional role obligation. However, this seems to commit the naturalistic fallacy in confusing the expectations that come with a role with one's obligations when exercising it.

Because of the heavy weather encountered by radical separatism, many commentators have opted for a more modest separatism in which professional role obligations are derived from morality, though sometimes indirectly, even if they are distinct from the obligations that one might have in everyday, noninstitutionalized contexts. Here a broad distinction can be made between interpersonal and institutional approaches taken in the literature on this point. *Interpersonal* approaches focus on the unique relationship between professionals and those whom they serve (clients, patients, or the public) and argue that professional role obligations are created by the distinctive moral features of those relationships. For many in the interpersonal camp, professional role obligations are not really separate from morality at all, but rather emerge when ordinary morality is applied in extraordinary circumstances.

Institutional approaches begin with an analysis of professions as social institutions, which play an important, if not necessary, role in the functioning of broader social systems, and then derive professional role obligations from the functional imperatives of those institutions. It is then argued that because the professions serve a unique role within social systems, professionals have unique role obligations.

Both interpersonal and institutional approaches begin with the basic claim that the distinctive nature of professional roles accounts for the unusual obligations that emerge in professional practice. To understand what is unique about the professions, either in terms of the distinctive relationships they create or the social functions that serve as their defining ends, it is worth understanding what constitutes a profession.

WHAT IS A PROFESSION?

The idea of a "profession" was developed in the medieval period with the rise of the university. At that time, three "learned professions" were recognized: law, medicine and divinity. But what was unique about these occupations? Unlike many other occupations, law, medicine and divinity required formal, standardized, and highly intellectual training. At this time "philosophy" by and large meant the study of theoretical and practical (moral) knowledge, and included the natural science (aka natural philosophy), logic, mathematics, rhetoric, ethics, metaphysics, and the like. University study at what today is called the "undergraduate" level was essentially the study of philosophy broadly understood. The specialized schools or colleges of the university were devoted to the learned professions: the schools of law, medicine, and divinity, respectively. The learned professions stood at the crossroads between *sophia* and *techne*—between abstract, intellectual knowledge, and applied skilled craft.

Many of the core characteristics of the medieval learned professions are still considered essential properties of any occupation rightfully called a profession. Today professions are occupations that offer effective expert assistance to society which: (1) require extensive training, (2) have a significant intellectual component, (3) provide an important service to society, (4) are organized into associations, and (5) articulate technical and ethical standards of competent professional practice.[7]

"Formal" professions, such as law and medicine, also have (6) credentialing or licensing requirements that limit who may engage in a particular professional practice. For instance, the legal community serves as a gatekeeper for entrance into the profession by working with state regulatory agencies to create and enforce credentialing and licensing standards that limit entry into the field. As a result, bona fide members of the profession enjoy (7) a monopoly on the market of their expert services. Formal professions such as law and medicine also enjoy (8) extensive self-governance in determining the technical and ethical standards of competent professional practice.

More "informal" professions have some, but not all of the qualities of the formal professions. Journalism, for instance, has a significant intellectual component, requires a certain measure of expertise, and serves a valuable social service. However, it lacks formal training, credentialing, and licensing requirements. "Anyone" can be journalist in a way that is not true for more formal professions. The distinction between formal and informal professions should be understood as a continuum as opposed to a strict bifurcation. Some professions, law and medicine being the chief examples, are paradigmatically formal. Some fields in engineering and accounting are also quite formal. However, most professions do not possess all eight characteristics of the formal professions and fall somewhere on the broad continuum between the paradigmatically formal professions on the one hand, and nonprofessional occupations on the other.

The professions, especially the more formal ones, are unique social institutions empowered with significant influence on important social services, systems, and markets. Professional practice, as an offer of expert assistance, also creates distinct relationships between professionals and the clients, patients, or members of the publics they serve. In explaining the distinctive nature of professional role obligations, interpersonal approaches to professional ethics focus on the unique qualities of the professional-client relationship and derive professional role obligations from the moral demands created by that relationship. Institutional approaches to professional ethics, on the other hand, focus on the unique function that the professions play in broader social systems. While there are a variety of attractive interpersonal and institutional approaches to professional ethics, there is good reason to believe that neither approach alone explains the distinct nature of professional role obligations. Interpersonal approaches tend to be incomplete because they are unable to explain why professional roles should exist in their current form. Institutional approaches provide powerful accounts for the features of contemporary professional roles, but ultimately offer the wrong sorts of reasons for understanding the obligations that professionals have to those whom they serve. The weaknesses of the two approaches can be illustrated by considering the difficulties encountered by interpersonal approaches to professional ethics that focus on promising, and institutional approaches that focus on collective responsibility.

INTERPERSONAL APPROACHES: PROMISING AND PROFESSIONAL ETHICS

One popular way of explaining the existence of special obligations is *volunteerism*. From this standpoint, special obligations are created by the voluntary, binding agreements made between individuals. Occupying a social role can therefore create special role obligations provided that the role-player has made a binding agreement—a promise or contract—to adhere to certain expectations. Professional role obligations gain their distinctive character because of the unique set of promises that professionals make via oaths, mission statements, and codes of ethics to one another and to those they serve.

A "promise" is a speech act by which a promisor communicates to a promisee that the promisor (1) has a firm intention to perform a certain action (ϕ) relevant to the promisee's interests, and (2) recognizes that in making such a communication, the promisor now has a compelling moral reason to ϕ, provided that the promisor is morally free to ϕ. Promising is an intuitive explanation for professional role obligations because promises routinely create special obligations that apply only to select individuals. For instance, from the standpoint of general morality, no one is obligated to watch Sara's dog while she is away for the weekend. However, if Bill *promises* to do so, then he invites a special vulnerability from Sarah who will now make action plans based on the assumption that Bill will honor his promise. Promises create the same kind of obligations in professions. Because professionals make promises to adhere to strict standards of conduct through their oaths, codes of ethics, and other communications, they acquire special obligations because they invite a unique vulnerability on the part of those they serve who now come to depend on the professional. The moral principle at play here is *fidelity* to one's promises, which is a widely accepted principle in ethics.

The promising approach seems to explain the existence of a distinct, yet morally grounded, professional ethics, and offers powerful moral reasons for why professionals obligations should be honored even when conflicting with everyday moral intuitions. Consider again Mark Pautler's deception of William Neal. However desirable his action might have been, the simple fact is that when he became a lawyer, Pautler promised, in his lawyer's oath and his acceptance of the legal profession's ethical rules conduct, to be rigorously honest in his professional activities—a promise he violated when he deceived Neal.

Some professions quite explicitly understand professional role obligations as being grounded in the promises professionals make to one another and to those they serve. Consider the American Pharmacist Association code of ethics:

> A pharmacist has moral obligations in response to the gift of trust received from society. In return for this gift, a pharmacist promises to help individuals achieve optimum benefit from their medications, to be committed to their welfare, and to maintain their trust. [8]

The general practice of requiring professionals to take oaths or pledges also seems to support the idea that promising plays an important role in normativity of the special rights and duties of professionals. Indeed, the word "profession" gains its meaning from the idea that the practitioner promises, or "professes," in an oath to uphold the service ideal of the practice.

Limitations of the Promising Approach to Professional Ethics

While an attractive way to understand professional obligations, the promising approach is not without its detractors. The criticisms of the view can be grouped into two broad objections. First, the promising approach offers no ethical guidance on the content of the promises that professionals ought to make to clients or the general public. Second, the kinds of commitments that professionals make to clients and the public are often very implicit and informal. Describing such implicit commitments as promises over-burdens the concept of promising.

The first objection runs something like this. While promises may explain how the cluster of norms of a given professional role become obligatory, they cannot explain what those norms should be in the first place.[9] Professionals might promise to respect client confidentiality, but why should they do so? Here the promising approach runs into something of a dilemma. On the one hand, if the professional has an obligation to make such a promise, then it appears the promising approach is not the source of professional role obligations; rather the source must be the underlying duties to make those promises. On the other hand, if professionals have no obligation to make certain promises, then one is left with an ungrounded account of professional ethics. Would it be morally acceptable for a profession, say, medicine, to announce that it would no longer promise to respect confidentiality? Most commentators (and patients!) would argue that such a profession would be unethical. If they are right, then it seems that promising—at least on its own—cannot explain the source of professional role obligations.

A second common objection to the promising approach focuses on the adequacy of promising as a description of the way professionals make interpersonal commitments to clients or the public. Professionals rarely, if ever, make formal, explicit promises to clients. Even for those who take oaths, and not all professionals do, such oaths are often presented as personal commitments and not necessarily as promises. If they are promises, promises to whom? Clients and the public might not be aware of the content of a professional's oath, or if the professional even took one. Moreover, while there is no doubt that professionals make a variety of representations to the clients and the public that are rightly thought of as implicit commitments, it strains the idea of promising to describe these commitments as promises.[10] Recall that a promise is a speech act in which a promisor communicates a firm intention to action ϕ, as well as a recognition that the speech act morally binds the promisor to ϕ. While oaths might be promises, many of the informal forms of communication made by professionals seem to fall short of the strict idea of what makes a particular speech act a promise.

These potential problems with the promising approach have led some commentators to argue that not only is the promising approach incomplete, it is essentially superfluous.[11] For these commentators, professional role obligations can be explained entirely by appeal to the unique social role played by professional institutions.

Institutional Approaches: Teleology and Professional Ethics

Institutional accounts of professional ethics derive professional role obligations from the rationale behind the institutionalization of the professional role. One of best institutional accounts comes from Alexandra and Miller's "teleological" account of professional ethics.[12] To show how professional roles are morally structured, Alexandra and Miller offer a rational reconstruction of professional roles that aims to show that the *telos*, or "definitive end," of the professions is not simply the promotion of the public interest, but more specifically the satisfaction of "fundamental needs." A fundamental need, in their account, is a need that, if not satisfied, entails significant harm.

Fundamental needs, according to Alexandra and Miller, create moral rights and corresponding duties to beneficence when an agent (S): (1) has a fundamental need, (2) which S cannot satisfy him or herself, and (3) which another agent (P) can satisfy for S without significant costs to P. Alexandra and Miller defend this view by appealing to intuitive and well-known "duty to rescue" cases. If while hiking, P encounters S in a life-threatening situation, and can assist S with no significant risk or costs, then it is widely held that P has a duty to assist S. These kinds of examples are common in ethical literature and, while not without critics, are uncontroversial.

Their next move, and the crux of their argument, is to extend the duty to assist to the institutional level and apply it to professional roles. In modern society, individuals will have various fundamental needs (e.g., basic levels of health, education, and safety), which they cannot satisfy themselves. For most individuals, satisfying fundamental needs requires the assistance of others who are knowledgeable and skilled in servicing that need. Because of this, Alexandra and Miller argue that modern communities have a *collective responsibility* to provide for the reliable satisfaction of fundamental needs. For instance, to satisfy the fundamental need for basic levels of health care, modern communities create hospitals and establish protocols for the proper training and vetting of health-care providers. The establishment of the medical profession is not simply done for the sake of efficiency, but helps fulfill the community's collective responsibility to provide for the reliable satisfaction of the fundamental need for health. The medical professions, in turn, create rules and standards of conduct that also reflect the telos or unique function of the professional role. Doctors are required to maintain confidentiality of patients because such confidentiality promotes the reliability of the profession's goal of meeting the health needs of the community. Far from being the results of promises, on this account, the professional role obligations "are actually institutional specifications and instantiations of the underlying collective responsibility to the needy."[13] By making professional rights and duties essential to the role itself, Alexandra and Miller conclude that individuals assume those obligations simply by occupying that role. One simply cannot *be* a doctor without being obligated by the norms of medical ethics, because those norms are necessary to satisfy the collective responsibility to provide adequate levels of health.

Limitations of Institutional Approaches

Institutional approaches to professional ethics such as Alexandra and Miller's teleological account offer a powerful explanation for the distinct nature of professional ethics by linking the moral and functional imperatives of the professional role. Of course, an account such as Miller and Alexandra's is also quite controversial. It entails a commitment to an extensive view of beneficence; the idea of *collective* responsibility; and the claim that individuals have a *right* to professional services. One could object that their conception of beneficence is relentlessly broad, that moral responsibility rests with persons, not collectives, and that professionals do not always service fundamental needs. These are serious objections to their approach, but perhaps the most significant limitation to their approach, and to institutional approaches generally, is that they give the wrong sorts of reasons for why professionals have obligations toward those whom they serve. This becomes clear when one considers the reasons to which clients, patients and the public appeal when they have been wronged by professional misconduct.

Consider the case of the "gossiping plastic surgeon." Suppose a patient gets treatments for cosmetic, plastic surgery. Cosmetic enhancements are usually not, according to Alexandra and Miller, a fundamental need.[14] Even so, by occupying the role "surgeon," the physician has a variety of obligations to the patient because the role has been designed to effectively meet the collective responsibility to satisfy the aggregate of fundamental needs in society. Suppose now the surgeon violates confidentiality and embarrasses the patient by disclosing intimate information about him or her. For Alexandra and Miller, doing so would be wrong because it undermines the effectiveness of the role "surgeon" in fulfilling its institutional function. The surgeon would be failing in his or her part in promoting the collective responsibility to make reliable health care available to the public.

While such a view is sensible enough, it does not offer the right sort of reasons for why the surgeon has wronged *this patient.* This is most clearly seen in the reactive attitudes that such a patient would have to the gossiping surgeon. Far from seeing the surgeon's duty as part of the "institutional specifications and instantiations of the underlying collective responsibility to the needy," the wronged patient will experience reactive attitudes of *personal* betrayal rooted in the idea that the surgeon was directly accountable to the patient. Such a patient would likely hold the surgeon accountable by saying something like "you hurt me" or "you betrayed my trust," rather than offering a complaint rooted in the society's collective responsibility.

Such reactive attitudes are by no means limited to cases in which fundamental rights are not being served. Consider the horrific case of Farad Fata, the oncologist who defrauded hundreds of patients by recommending aggressive cancer treatments they did not need. During his sentencing, victims were offered the opportunity to testify about the wrong done to them, and their statements centered on the *interpersonal* reasons that Fata was accountable. Said one patient, "I gave full and total trust to this man to get me and my family through this journey I was about to begin. . . . Dr. Fata took full advantage of my trust in him, my fear of dying and, most of all, my top of the line health insurance"[15] Indeed, Fata himself cited the interpersonal nature of his obligation in his apology to his victims: "I have violated the Hippocratic oath and violated the trust of my patients."[16]

PROFESSIONAL ROLE OBLIGATIONS AND THE SECOND-PERSON STANDPOINT

The reactive attitudes of those wronged by professional misconduct suggest that the reasons why professionals are accountable to those they serve are ultimately interpersonal and not institutional. Of course, it could be the case that these reactive attitudes are merely psychological reactions to harm, and that when one thinks rigorously about the rational source of what persons owe one another, one is lead to a more institutional theory of obligation. However, a wide variety of ethicists argue that this is not so—that the reactive attitudes of persons when wronged point to the fact that the source of moral obligation is ultimately interpersonal.

Stephan Darwall, for instance, argues in *The Second-Person Standpoint* that moral accountability is made possible by the fact that persons can claim a practical authority over one another and demand certain treatment, or justifications for treatments, in light of one's standing as a free and equal member of the moral community.[17] For instance, when having his or her foot stepped on, a person might say, "please don't do that," thus asserting an authority to demand accountability on the other. When someone wrongs another person intentionally, the reactive attitudes of the victim—resentment, indignation, betrayal, and the like—are rooted in the fact that persons qua persons are uniquely accountable to one another. It is not rational to be resentful about the gloomy weather—weather is not accountable to persons. It is rational, on the other hand, for a person to resent someone who intentionally harms or takes advantage of his or her vulnerabilities.

Moral accountability; that is, holding others accountable in light of what one thinks is owed to them, emerges in what Darwall calls the "second-person standpoint"—an engaged, will-to-will, or I-Thou, relationship marked by mutual recognition of each other's status as *persons.* When holding others accountable, persons rightly demand second-person reasons for the justification of treatment they find objectionable; reasons that are rooted in the dignity of persons that should be honored as free and equal members of the moral community. The reactive attitudes of wronged patients, clients, and

members of the public are therefore not simply emotional reactions to perceived harm; they are *demands for accountability* rooted in the second-
person standpoint.

Moral accountability is intrinsically, and perhaps dialectically, related to
moral obligation. For instance, when an agent holds another accountable and
blames him or her for immoral conduct, the agent is referencing a moral
obligation. Darwall cites Mill's comment that "we do not call anything
wrong unless we mean to imply that a person ought to be punished in some
way or other for doing it," either by law, the criticisms and social sanction of
others, or "the reproaches of his own conscience."[18] Or, as Darwall puts it,
"there can be no such thing as a moral obligation and wrongdoing without
the normative standing to demand and hold agents accountable for compliance."[19]

Because accountability and obligation are dialectically related—they are
the preconditions for one another—the second-person standpoint plays an
important role in the kind of reasons that ground obligations. Obligations
need to be understood in the context of the second-person standpoint and the
mutual recognition of personhood that is inherent in such a perspective. For
this reason, moral obligations must be justified on the grounds of what is
owed to the other as a free and equal member of the moral community who
has the authority to hold one accountable for acting in a manner consistent
with that status. As a result, moral justifications rooted in the efficient production of a certain state of affairs, even a morally desirable state of affairs,
are the wrong kinds of reasons for holding others morally accountable. Obligations need to be justified in ways that are indigenous to the second-person
standpoint if they are to offer the right sorts of reasons—second-person reasons—for why person can be held morally accountable.

Darwall's point is nicely illustrated by thinking about the wrong committed by enslaving another human being. Utilitarianism has often been criticized for allowing for the possibility of a just institution of slavery provided
that it creates the greatest happiness for the greatest number of people. Bent-
ham argued that this could not be so—that the pain created by slavery is so
intense that the institution would never achieve net social utility. Even if one
granted this point, one cannot help but ask: is the wrong of slavery really
located in its net disutility for society? Or rather, does its wrong lie in the
failure to extend the dignity that ought to be accorded to all persons qua
persons? Surely the slave does not cry out, "You create disutility by treating
me this way!" Rather, the slave cries, "I am not an object, but a human
being!" As persons generally would not grant permission to others to enslave
them, they must accord to others the same dignity; or, as Lincoln put it, "As I
would not be a slave, so I would not be a master."[20]

This same problem plagues institutional accounts of professional ethics.
While it may be morally desirable to construct professional roles in a particu-

lar manner, and while doing so may satisfy broader collective responsibilities, these accounts fail to offer the kind of second-person reasons that explain why professionals are accountable to the specific persons they serve. When a professional wrongs a client or patient, the blameworthiness is not exclusively, or even primarily, due to the professional's failure to promote the collective responsibility to satisfy fundamental needs. Rather, the primary blameworthiness of wronging those served by the professional lies in its violation of the client or patient as persons. It is for this, second-person reason, that wronged clients appeal to betrayed trust, promise breaking, or inhumane treatment when holding professional misconduct blameworthy.

A THIRD WAY: TRUST AS MEDIATING THE INTERPERSONAL AND INSTITUTIONAL

Interpersonal accounts of professional ethics such as the promising approach rightly offer second-person reasons for professional accountability, but fail to sufficiently anchor which specific obligations the professional should promise to uphold. Moreover, promising may be too specific a practice to account for the variety of implicit ways that professionals make commitments to those they serve. On the other hand, while the institutional approach explains why it is desirable, perhaps even morally desirable, for professionals to adopt certain standards of conduct, it fails to give the right kinds of reasons that show why professionals are morally accountable *specifically* to the persons they serve.

An adequate approach to professional ethics must integrate institutional and interpersonal considerations if it is to explain both the distinct nature of professional role obligations, and why those obligations are *owed* to those served by professions. One possible way of mediating these approaches, and the one developed in this book, is to ground professional role obligations in the reasons professionals have to invite, develop, and honor the trust of those they serve. Like promising, trust is an interpersonal moral phenomenon and generates second-person reasons rooted in an I-Thou relationship between persons. Indeed, for some ethicists, promises are a kind of invitation to trust. Moreover, trust seems to be a key element in both the reactive attitudes of wronged clients, such as Dr. Fata's victims, and in the motivation of virtuous professionals committed to honoring the trust they have invited from those they serve. At the same time, trust is well known in the social sciences as a key element in the functioning of social institutions.[21] Indeed, ethicists have only recently come around to the study of trust as a moral concept. Before that, trust was the province of social scientists who saw it as a mechanism that accounted for the stability of practices and complex social institutions.

Trust-Based Professional Ethics: The Main Ideas

Trust-based professional ethics begins with the relatively weak claim that the telos professional practice generally is *an offer of effective expert assistance.* Accepting such an offer entails a variety of vulnerabilities for patients, clients, employers, and even the public. Professional-client relationships are marked by often-unavoidable knowledge and power asymmetries. Those who rely on professionals entrust important interests—in many cases fundamental needs—to the discretionary decision-making of the professional. Because patients, clients, or the public cannot closely police the professional's work, they must *trust* the professional. Trust is the coin of the realm of professional practice. When trust is insufficient, clients and patients deploy a variety of *hedging* strategies to limit their vulnerability, but these very strategies limit the effectiveness of the professional service. For instance, patients with low levels of trust in their physician are less likely to seek medical assistance, less likely to be forthcoming about their condition, less likely to follow through on treatment plans, and more likely to perceive treatment outcomes as negative ones. Additionally, the public's trust in professional communities is essential to the support for social arrangements by which the formal professionals are given self-governing monopolies on key social services.

Trust is essential to effective professional practice, but that does not alone prove that professions have an *obligation* to invite and develop client trust. The efficiency of practices alone does not provide the second-person reasons necessary to make them obligatory. The professional's obligation to invite and develop trust is rooted in the respect for the personhood of the client, patient, and general public. Professionals are given a wide variety of social capital, ranging from increased prestige to monopolistic control of social services. In return, those served by professionals reasonably expect effective expert assistance. The idea of reciprocal justice or "fair play"[22] requires that professionals honor their end of this "social bargain" and engage in the practices necessary for their expert assistance to be effective, which, in this case, includes inviting and developing client trust.

Professionals have an obligation to invite and develop the trust of those whom they serve. Given the important needs entrusted to their care, professionals invite trust by making a variety of explicit and implicit fiduciary commitments. They invite trust on the grounds that they can be relied upon, among other things, to be uniquely honest, loyal, respectful of client autonomy, discreet and diligent. In inviting a trusting dependence from those they serve, professionals have an obligation to honor their fiduciary commitments as a matter of respect for the unique vulnerability they have invited from those who trust them.

Because they have an obligation to invite, develop, and honor the trust of those whom they serve, professionals, by extension, have an obligation to be *trustworthy*. Clients form trust in professionals in part because they infer that professionals are trustworthy. Professionals who are not trustworthy will not be able to develop trust, or will to do so through unethical deception. To be trustworthy, professionals must, among other things, develop the personal traits necessary to reliably care for the interests entrusted to them. Integrity, loyalty, honesty, respect for autonomy, discretion, beneficence, and diligence are therefore not only fiduciary commitments—promises, if you will—that professionals make to those who depend on them, they are *professional virtues* that professionals must develop in their own character.

Being trustworthy is necessary to develop an ethical basis for trust with clients, but it is not sufficient. Professionals must be *effectively trustworthy*— that is, they must not only possess the professional virtues that make them reliable, they must also effectively signal or communicate that trustworthiness to (would-be) dependents. Impression and signal management is not only a good business strategy; it is necessary if the professional is to develop client and public trust.

Developing the professional virtues and being effectively trustworthy highlight the important role of the profession as an *ethical community*. As ethical communities, the professions maintain ongoing ethical/existential, moral, and application discourses that are oriented to interpreting the professional telos and the obligations necessary to responsibly care for the vulnerability of those they serve. Professional communities link these discourses with educational practices that aim at developing the professional virtues among their members, and credentialing and compliance standards that offer institutional incentives for responsible conduct. Finally, community members make intersubjective commitments to one another, sometimes dramatically in the form of oaths, to uphold the obligations inherent in the profession's practice.

The profession-as-ethical-community plays an important role in the effective signaling of the professional's trustworthiness by developing and promulgating the reputation of the professional social-type. Because those who depend on professionals often have little, if any, personal familiarity with them, they depend on the reputation of the professional role in extending *anonymous trust* to professionals. When inviting anonymous trust, professionals utilize the reputation of their professional role as a "bootstrapping" mechanism to initiate trust development with clients. Reputation of the professional role works dialectically with professional's impression management, and the ethical quality of one's professional conduct. Given the importance of reputation, professionals are also accountable to their peers because their own conduct influences the overall professional reputation. When professionals engage in misconduct, they not only wrong their clients or patients, they also wrong fellow members of the professional community by damaging the reputation of the professional role.

Trust-Based Professional Ethics and the Pautler Case

How would trust-based professional ethics apply to the case of Mark Pautler—the prosecutor who pretended to be a public defender in order to apprehend a murderer? It might be tempting to think that an exclusively teleological approach would be sufficient to explain his unique role obligation to honesty. Lawyers serve the fundamental need for justice, and honesty is a requirement of servicing that need. But Pautler could (and did!) argue that if the goal of the legal profession is to promote justice, surely honesty must at least *occasionally* give way to other norms, such as efficiency in capturing dangerous criminals. Paulter argued that his deception of Neal actually promoted the defining end of the legal profession.

The Colorado Supreme Court, which, on the recommendation of the Colorado State Bar, suspended Pautler's license to practice law, took a dramatically different tack. It held that honesty was one of the core traits of the trustworthy lawyer. For that reason, lawyers are rightly held to rigorous standards of honest conduct despite the noble ends that might be served by deception. This is reflected in the Model Rules of Professional Conduct for the Colorado State Bar which state: "It is professional misconduct for a lawyer to: (c) engage in conduct involving dishonesty, fraud, deceit or misrepresentation."[23] The Court took note of the rigorous, almost categorical nature of this rule:

> No exception to the prohibition contained in Colo. RPC 8.4(c) is found within the rules nor is any suggested within the explanatory commentary. After exhaustive research, not a single case has been discovered which recognizes an exception to the ethical principle that a lawyer may not engage in deceptive conduct.[24]

It is no accident that lawyers are held to such a rigorous standard of honesty. The legal profession serves the public interest of preserving and promoting justice and as such, it plays a vital role in the preservation of society itself. Individual clients create a significant personal vulnerability by taking up the lawyer's invitation to trust. Moreover, the legal profession enjoys broad self-governance in its monopolization of legal services. Such self-governance requires an extension of significant trust from the general public to the legal profession. For these reasons, lawyers make clear—dramatically clear in their oath, but also in their model rules of professional conduct—that they can be trusted on the grounds that they will be, among other things, honest with those who depend on them. These commitments are an important way in which the profession develops the reputation of the professional role. Were lawyers not to make such commitments, they would not be able to effectively offer expert assistance to clients and the public at large, thus exploiting the benefits of their role without doing their fair share to promote its core value.

In addition, the Court concluded that, even among lawyers, Paulter had distinctive, and more stringent, professional obligations given his unique role as a prosecutor:

> Prosecutors, who are enforcers of the law, have higher ethical duties than other lawyers because they are ministers of justice, not just advocates. . . . They must be forever vigilant that their conduct as attorneys not only meets the minimum standards of conduct set forth in The Rules of Professional Conduct but they must strive to exceed those requirements. They must also carefully carry out their duty to protect the public in the exercise of their prosecutorial responsibilities while maintaining the duties and responsibilities of professional conduct imposed upon them by The Rules of Professional Conduct. They may not choose to satisfy the former at the expense of the latter. [25]

However noble his intention, Paulter *exploited* his role by taking advantage of the trusting expectations created by the fiduciary commitments made by lawyers, including Paulter himself, and the role reputation developed by the legal community. His personal representations to Neal were nothing short of an invitation to trust based on those commitments. Pautler was therefore obligated to honor, as in a promise, the trust he had secured from Neal. If he was not willing to do so, then he should not have invited that trust. When instead he used that invited trust to deceive the "client" he pretended to serve, he wronged Neal by exploiting his trust. The bona fide public defender later assigned to Neal complained of the difficulty in creating a trusting relationship with him once Pautler's ruse had been exposed. Neal eventually dismissed his public defender and represented himself at trial.

Pautler also wronged his peers. Given the importance of the professional reputation, lawyers make a commitment to one another that they will reliably conduct themselves in a manner that promotes the reputation of the profession. A lawyer offering to assist a "client," and then using that trust for the purpose of deception, strikes at the very heart of the reputation of the professional role. Paulter made a commitment to his peers that he would be honest in his professional conduct, a commitment he breached when he deceived and manipulated Neil. In doing so he also hurt himself by diminishing his personal reputation for trustworthiness among his peers.

There are, of course, limits to one's obligation to honor trust and keep one's commitments. For instance, there is no moral obligation to keep a promise if doing so requires immoral behavior. Pautler argued that his case constituted just such an exception—and it is here that a certain measure of reasonable disagreement about the Pautler case has emerged. Pautler argued that his deception of Neal was *necessary* to protect the public from an imminent threat and that he was therefore obligated to do so. If correct, this would justify his dishonesty. While there is a *prima facie* obligation to honor trust, those obligations can be trumped by other, more important obligations. Because he was morally required to deceive Neal, Pautler argued, he was freed from his duty to honor Neal's trust.

The Colorado Supreme Court rejected Pautler's argument, in fact, though not in principle. In this case, the court held that the fact the sheriff had already made an effort to contact *another* defense lawyer indicated that the subsequent deception of Neil was unnecessary. If one defense attorney had already been sought at Neal's request, why not simply seek out another?

Pautler also argued that, while perhaps not necessary, the threat to public safety was significant enough to make his deception morally desirable. The court rejected this view because of the slippery slope such a principle would create. If Pautler were allowed to lie, even for noble intent and under extreme conditions, then the door is opened for less scrupulous lawyers to find/invent pretexts that would justify an increasing range of dishonesty. Dishonest behavior on the part of lawyers discredits the profession and the justice system itself, so clients, the public, and even lawyers themselves, have good reasons to insist on categorical honesty among lawyers, even in extreme cases. To invite and develop the trust of clients and the public, lawyers make a "zealous" commitment to honesty—even in cases in which such a commitment does not serve the public interest in the immediate instance. It is for these reasons that Pautler was required to follow rules of conduct requiring honesty in professional conduct.

CONCLUSION

The Pautler case illustrates how professionals have a variety of role-based obligations that are quite distinct from those in everyday interactions. Interpersonal and institutional accounts are each too limited to provide a satisfactory explanation for the distinct nature of professional role obligations and are best brought into a dialectical relationship via the mediating concept of trust. The telos of a given profession elucidates the range of trust that should be invited and developed from patients, clients, and the general public. Once invited, professionals have an obligation rooted in the idea of fidelity to honor the trust extended to them. Because client-professional relationships are unusual in that they occur under relatively anonymous conditions, those who depend on professionals entrust important interests to their discretionary judgment in a relationship characterized by knowledge and power asymmetries. Professionals must invite and develop an unusual form of trust, and therefore have unusual obligations when honoring that trust.

NOTES

1. *People v. Pautler* 47 P.3d 1175, 1184 (Colo. 2002).

2. Bernard Gert and Charles Culver, *Bioethics: A Systematic Approach* (Oxford, UK: Oxford University Press, 2006).

3. *Code of Conduct for United States Judges*, accessed May 10, 2016, http://www.uscourts.gov/judges-judgeships/code-conduct-united-states-judges#d

4. Benjamin Freedman, "A Meta-ethics for Professional Morality," *Ethics* 89 (1978): 19.

5. John-Christian Smith, "Strong Separatism in Professional Ethics. Professional Ethics," *Professional Ethics* 3 (1994): 117–40.

6. Alan Gewirth, "Professional Ethics: The Separatist Thesis," *Ethics* 96 (1986): 286.

7. Michael Bayles, *Professional Ethics.* 2nd ed. (Belmont, CA: Wadsworth, 1989), 7–13.

8. "Code of Ethics for Pharmacists," American Pharmacist Association, accessed August 13, 2015, http://www.pharmacist.com/code-ethics.

9. Andrew Alexandra and Seamus Miller, *Ethics in Practice: Moral Theory and the Professions* (Kesington, AUS: University of New South Wales Press, 2009), 105.

10. For instance, see Michael Davis, "Thinking Like an Engineer: The Place of a Code of Ethics in the Practice of a Profession," *Philosophy and Public Affairs* 20 (1991): 150–167.

11. Alexandra and Miller, *Ethics in Practice: Moral Theory and the Professions*, 105.

12. See Alexandra and Miller, "Needs, Moral Consciousness and Professional Roles," *Professional Ethics* 5 (1996): 43–61; Alexandra and Miller, "Ethical Theory, 'Common Morality,' and Professional Obligations," *Theoretical Medicine and Bioethics* 30 (2009): 69–80; and Alexandra and Miller, *Ethics in Practice: Moral Theory and the Professions.*

13. Alexandra and Miller, *Ethics in Practice: Moral Theory and the Professions*, 80.

14. Alexandra and Miller, "Needs, Moral Self-Consciousness, and Professional Roles," 55.

15. "Patients Give Horror Stories as Cancer Doctor Gets 45 Years" CNN, accessed August 20, 2015, http://www.cnn.com/2015/07/10/us/michigan-cancer-doctor-sentenced/

16. Ibid.

17. Stephan Darwall, *The Second-Person Standpoint: Morality, Respect and Accountability.* (Cambridge, MA: Harvard University Press, 2006).

18. Darwall, *The Second-Person Standpoint*, 92.

19. Darwall, *The Second-Person Standpoint*, 99.

20. Abraham Lincoln, *Speeches and Writings, 1832–1858*, ed. Don Fehrenbacher (New York: Library of America, 1989): 484.

21. See Harold Garfinkel. "A Conception of, and Experiments with 'Trust' as a Condition of Stable Concerted Action." In *Motivation and Social Interaction*, ed. O.J. Harvey. New York: The Ronald Press, 1963; Niklas Luhmann, *Trust and Power* (Chichester: John Wiley & Sons, 1979)

22. John Rawls, *A Theory of Justice* (Cambridge, MA: Belknap Press, 1999): 93–98.

23. *People v. Pautler.*

24. Ibid.

25. Ibid.

Chapter Two

Vulnerability and Trust in the Professions

Trust-based professional ethics locates the source of professional role obligations in the unique nature of the client-professional relationship, a relationship structured by the professional telos. When professionals, both as individuals and as members of professional communities, invite the trust of clients, patients, students, and the general public, they have an obligation to honor that trust, thus creating, as in the case of promising, unique obligations not shared by the general public. Professional ethics is not as much a separate ethical system as it is ordinary morality applied to extraordinary, trusting relationships.

But what is trust? And why should professionals *invite* the trust of those they serve? Professional service entails risk and vulnerability on the part of clients and the public because of the knowledge and power asymmetries typically present in client-professional relationships. Trust is essential for professional practice precisely because it is the attitude in which one is willing to make oneself vulnerable to the discretionary choices of another person. The development of trust is a functional imperative of professional practice—it simply would not work without trust. However, professionals also have good ethical and moral reasons to invite and develop trust. Ethically, the development of trust promotes the flourishing of professionals in light of the defining goal, or telos, of the profession. Morally, the development of trust is necessary if the professional is to form second-person, "I-Thou" relationships with clients and patients, and justly satisfy their "social bargain" with the general public.

KNOWLEDGE AND POWER ASYMMETRIES IN THE PROFESSIONAL PRACTICE

It has been widely argued that the professional-client relationship is a *fiduciary* one.[1] Understood broadly, a fiduciary relationship occurs when individual S entrusts P with discretionary power over an important interest.[2] By accepting this discretionary power, P has an obligation to responsibly promote that interest. In the professional context, those who rely on the expertise of professionals (e.g., clients, patients, students, the public) entrust them with discretionary power to promote important interests. In accepting this authorization, professionals take on the responsibility to promote those interests.

Granting such discretionary power entails risk, potentially great risk. Patients entrust their health to their physicians, while clients entrust their legal well-being, perhaps even their freedom, to their lawyer. Accountants and financial professionals are entrusted with one's financial well-being, while engineers and architects are entrusted with one's personal safety, as well as the safety of the public. Such reliance is by no means, or even primarily, limited to professions who serve clients directly. The expertise required to manage complex social systems requires the public to rely routinely on the discretionary authority of professions. Judges and prosecutors are entrusted with preserving law and order in the name of "the people," public administrators are charged with the efficient management of core governmental systems, while engineers promote the safety of members of the public they will never meet.

Reliance on the discretionary choices of another person creates vulnerability, but in professional practice such vulnerability is exacerbated by the knowledge and power asymmetries between professionals and those they serve. Professionals offer expertise lacked by those who depend on them. For this reason, it is simply not possible for the typical client to police the work done by the professional. Patients, for instance, entrust physicians with their health and lack both the expertise and access to check and confirm the work the physician performs for them. While patients can in some cases seek out a "second opinion" on major recommendations from a physician, this is not plausible for every decision the physician makes. Moreover, appealing to a second opinion creates a reliance on yet another physician under similar conditions of risk and knowledge asymmetry. Even sophisticated clients, such as banks and investment firms, are vulnerable to the knowledge asymmetries between themselves and the professionals who serve them. This was demonstrated in the 2009 financial crisis when banks and investment firms depended on the integrity of financial professionals rating mortgage securities. Because the securities were rated inaccurately, sophisticated agents (as well as general members of the public) invested in financial products that were essentially worthless. Even employers, while having more control over their professionals than do clients or the public, need to rely on professional expertise in ways that create organizational risk, such as when trade secrets need to be shared with engineers so they may improve technological processes.

Many professional relationships are also characterized by important asymmetries of power. The physician in a hospital is a powerful figure within a complex institution with the ability to navigate the system and command the respect of its members. Patients, on the other hand, are typically "outsiders" to this system, and not only lack knowledge of its intimate workings, but also have very little influence on it. As Max Weber observed, social systems, particularly bureaucratic ones, are often designed precisely to buffer the influence of external forces.[3] For a social system such as a hospital, patients are external inputs that need to be "processed" according to system procedures. The physician, on the other hand, is an indigenous "player" in the system wielding considerable procedural and informal power. Patients and their families do, of course, influence the system, but they lack the formal and informal power of an "insider," and are thus often forced to "lay siege" to the system and reactively "counter steer" it.[4]

Sometimes the power asymmetry between professionals and those they serve is rooted in social class differences. As members of the expert class, professionals wield significant social capital that translates into symbolic power when interacting with others, particularly those from lower social classes who are relatively impoverished in terms of social capital. The still prevalent idea that "the doctor knows best" is not only rooted in the expertise of the physician, but in the social prestige, respect, and authority granted to the social role.

These asymmetries become even more acute when clients rely on professionals in times of personal crises. A patient recently diagnosed with a terminal illness, a client charged with a serious felony, or a business owner whose enterprise faces financial ruin must all rely on professionals under conditions of extreme duress. This duress can have a real impact on the decision-making capacity of the client, thus increasing his or her vulnerability.

Reliance on a professional comes with a variety of risks, undertaken under conditions of knowledge and power asymmetries, and under varying, and sometimes extreme, conditions of personal vulnerability. To make matters yet even more difficult, reliance on professionals typically occurs under relatively *anonymous* conditions. Clients typically rely on lawyers, physicians, therapists, accountants, and engineers with very little, if any, personal familiarity with them. When a client needing a certified public accountant seeks out the assistance of an accounting firm, he or she may know nothing about the accountant assigned to them save for the fact that the individual is a CPA (if they actually *know* that) working at that firm. The situation is all the more precarious for the public, which must rely on judges, prosecutors, administrators, engineers and a phalanx of other professionals with whom they have no personal contact.

Given these conditions, routine reliance on professionals is an astonishing social accomplishment. Those who depend on professions entrust important interests to anonymous individuals whose work they often cannot police. Given the distinct possibility of fraud and mistreatment, it is a wonder that rational agents come to trust professionals at all—yet they do, everyday (you are right now by reading this book). The very existence of the professions, and the routine reliance on them, is only possible given the development of a very special form of *trust*. Without the development of this trust, the professions simply could not exist.

WHAT IS TRUST?

While there is much debate about the nature of trust, there is broad agreement that trust involves: (1) a willingness to rely on the actions of another (2) in a way that creates vulnerability or risk (3) in light of an assumption that the other will act favorably toward one's interests.[5] There is also something special about trust that can be seen in the reactive attitudes expressed when it is violated. In the 1960s, social psychologist Harold Garfinkel was studying the underlying mechanisms of stable patterns of social interaction and devised a series of "breaching" experiments in which experimenters would violate mundane expectations or rules of social interaction. He had chess players rearrange the pieces in the middle of the game, family members act as if they were tenants renting a room, customers haggle over fixed priced items, and ordinary interlocutors challenge the meaning of mundane expressions.[6]

Garfinkel found that violations of the expectations of mundane behavior triggered reactive attitudes expressing not only surprise and frustration, but also *moral* indignation and betrayal. In some of the experiments, the subjects went so far as to question the moral character of the experimenter. This led Garfinkel to conclude that trust is a special kind of reliance in that it entails a *moral orientation* in which others are held *accountable* to "play by the rules." He characterized trust as a kind of implied contract or binding agreement between social actors.[7]

The fact that violations of trust create reactive *moral* attitudes such as blame, indignation, resentment, and a sense of betrayal provides insight into the objects, attitudes and warrants of trust. First, because the reactive attitudes are moral they indicate that trust involves an ascription of obligation to the trustee to responsibly care for entrusted interests. Thus violations of trust are not only disappointing, but also *blameworthy*. For this reason, trust has as its object only other moral agents. For instance, while one can trust a spouse, a doctor, and fellow drivers on the road, one cannot trust a house, a car, or the weather. In trust, one choses to *rely* on another moral agent and, in doing so, makes oneself vulnerable to that agent's will.

But not *all* reliance on others is trust. Immanuel Kant famously took his morning walk in his hometown of Königsberg so punctually that one could set one's watch to it.[8] Suppose one of Kant's neighbors, Jürgen, sends his children to school when Kant walks by. One day Kant is struggling to make a particular passage of *The Critique of Pure Reason* less opaque and foregoes his walk, and as a result Jürgen's children are late for school. While Jürgen has been injured due to his reliance on Kant, it would be inappropriate for him to feel moral indignation toward him. In this particular case, Jürgen's reliance on Kant was based on his predictability, not on the expectation that Kant would responsibly *care* for his interests. The former case is sometimes described as *confidence*—an optimistic attitude about an expected outcome based on the predictability of certain persons or processes.[9] The attitude Jürgen had toward Kant is confidence, as is the attitude one has toward a car when relying on it to start on a cold day. In trust, as opposed to confidence, one relies on the Other to show goodwill or care for an entrusted interest. In this kind of reliance, one assigns or ascribes an obligation for such goodwill or care,[10] and if the trustee fails to provide such care, then the reactive attitudes observed by Garfinkel—moral indignation and a sense of betrayal—are quite understandable.

But are such reactive attitudes rational? In other words, what is the justification for ascribing an obligation to those whom one trusts? Simply ascribing an obligation to another person does not *ipso facto* obligate them. One cannot simply will an obligation onto others. In the case of trust there are at least two grounds for rationally ascribing an obligation to the trustee: prior agreement and respect for vulnerability.

The clearest case of rational obligation ascription occurs when trust is grounded in prior agreement. For example, when trust is based on a promise, agents rightfully ascribe a fidelity obligation to the trustee to provide the promised care of one's interests. Fidelity to promises, contracts, and other binding agreements are among the most widely accepted principles in ethics, and can be justified from numerous moral frameworks. As Hume and Mill argued, a general rule requiring fidelity to such agreements promotes social utility by extending the range of cooperative behavior in the face of risk and uncertainty.[11] From more deontological perspectives, absent special circumstances, persons would reasonably refuse permission to others to manipulate their expectations by breaking one's agreements.

Ascriptions of obligations to trustees are by no means limited to situations of prior agreement. The most robust trusting relationships are with family and friends, and these relationships are not particularly well understood in terms of promising, contracts, or other prior agreements.[12] A seven-year-old boy trusts his mother and father in numerous ways to care for his well-being and safety, even in the absence of a promise or contract to do so. One could argue that parents make an implicit binding agreement with society to care for their children, but this offers the wrong sorts of reasons for moral accountability to one's children. Certainly the seven-year-old boy, if uncared for, will not cite an informal social contract in expressing his moral indignation. From the second-person standpoint, parents *engage* their child in an I-Thou relationship, and the moral accountability *to him* needs to be explicated in terms of reasons that are indigenous to that relationship. For this reason, the obligation to care for children is better rooted in the proper moral response to the unique vulnerability of children in relation to their parents. [13]

It is widely accepted that there is a general obligation of nonmalfeasance—to avoid harming others. Again from a wide variety of ethical perspectives one can justify a prima facie duty of nonmalfeasance in which, absent special circumstances, we ought to avoid harming others. Such a rule promotes social utility and respects the inherent dignity of one's fellow moral agents. When proposed actions will harm others, the prima facie duty of nonmalfeasance generally provides good reason to change one's plans. There are, of course, various contexts in which this obligation does not hold—harming others in self-defense, or in a context of prior consent (e.g., Fight Club or a hockey game) are common examples.

When someone trusts, they *en*trust someone the care of an important interest. [14] In doing so, they take a risk—they create a vulnerability by which they can be harmed by the discretion of the trustee. Because of the duty of nonmalfeasance, trust gives someone good reasons to act responsibly toward that vulnerability. Of course, trust does not provide an absolute reason to do so. There can be numerous situations in which there is no obligation to care for those that extend trust. Consider the infamous *Human Fund* from *Seinfield.* Suppose George reveals to a coworker that his charity—*The Human Fund*—is fake and he is systematically defrauding others by soliciting contributions to the fund. While George may have trusted his coworker, thus making himself vulnerable, the coworker has good reason to betray that trust.

Absent such special circumstances, the general obligation to responsibly care for others when they are uniquely vulnerable to one's actions makes it possible to trust others in the absence of prior agreements. If Laura and her friend Jeannette are at a park with their daughters and Laura has to take an important phone call, even without prior consent Laura might rationally trust Jeannette to watch after her daughter as she walks away to a quiet spot to take the call. In such a case, she ascribes to Jeannette an obligation to care for her vulnerability (the well-being of her daughter) because she believes it would be wrong for Jeannette to show indifference to the significant harm her actions (or inactions) could cause her. After all, if her daughter were missing when she returned, it would not be appropriate for Jeannette to say,

"I knew you were distracted, but because there was no prior agreement, I paid no attention to your daughter." Such a response would provoke indignation (and a search for a new friend).

As a moral orientation, trust is: (1) a willingness to rely on the discretion of a trustee (2) in a way that creates vulnerability for the trustor, and in which (3) the trustor ascribes an obligation to the trustee to responsibly care for one's interests either (a) due to prior agreement or (b) due to respect for the unique vulnerability of the trustor to the actions of the trustee.

The last thing to consider is the warrant for trust.[15] Trust is warranted when a trustor can rationally infer that a trustee is *trustworthy*—that is, that the trustee can be relied upon to responsibly care for trustor's unique vulnerability. When Laura received that phone call why would she trust Jeannette to note her vulnerability and watch her daughter in her absence? Likely she believed that her friends are generally good people who can be depended upon to promote her well-being. Had they been mere acquaintances, she probably would have created a prior agreement ("Will you watch my daughter while I am away?") before trusting her. Had they been complete strangers, she might have looked for signs of Jeanette's trustworthiness (e.g., being another parent with children, dress, behavior, mannerisms) before extending her trust.

This kind of example highlights the fact that the justified inference that someone is trustworthy, while rational, is not always, or even primarily, an intellectualized and deliberative process. The situation of Laura receiving a phone call requires her to make an intuitive judgment based on cognitive, normative, and affective features of the situation and of her relationship, or lack thereof, with Jeannette. To the degree she lacks a relationship with Jeannette, any trust Laura extends in this situation will require an intuitive feel for her. The way Jeannette presents herself in the situation will lead Laura to intuitively "slot" her into a social category and use this categorization to get a "feel" for her trustworthiness. The relationship between the social presentation of the trustee and the intuitions of the trustor is essential in many professional contexts in which those who rely on professionals extend *anonymous trust* to them. How professions need to present themselves to effectively (and affectively) elicit trust is discussed in more detail in chapter 5.

Trust, especially when formed swiftly and anonymously, requires a (sometimes rather intuitive) judgment about the trustworthiness of the trustee. Such judgments will not be based on perfect information conditions, and there always lurks the possibility of misplaced trust extended to charlatans who mimic trustworthiness. For this reason, Annette Baier, in her influential work on trust, argues that trust is an optimistic attitude about the character of a moral agent such that one expects them to responsibly care for that which is entrusted to them.[16] In short, trust is extended because the trustor believes the trustee is a "good" person and thus will be benevolent. This "moral" account of trust explains why Garfinkel found that violations of trust sometimes led subjects to reassess the moral character of the experimenter—to doubt if they were really "good" people.

A common objection to Baier's "moral" account of trust is that it would limit trust only to individuals who thought of one another as virtuous, which is empirically too narrow. Relatively immoral agents (e.g., drug dealers) routinely trust one another even though they have no illusions about each other's character.[17] However, the optimistic attitude adopted in trust need not depend on a global assessment of someone's character, but can be grounded on the specific elements of character relevant to the entrusted interest. Trust is rarely, if ever, extended to another person globally, but is extended to particular persons in specific action domains. This makes trust a "three part" phenomenon with a trustor, a trustee, and an action or action domain.[18] S trusts P to ϕ (or in action domain ϕ). So, even relatively immoral individuals can have grounds for trust because they can take an optimistic attitude about the trustee's goodwill based on the inference that the trustee possesses trust-warranting properties relative to specific action domains. As Plato pointed out in *The Republic*, while pirates are not particularly just persons, they at least must be just among themselves.

Some critics are still not satisfied. For them, it is possible to trust someone on completely amoral grounds. For instance, motorists trust others to drive responsibly, even though they lack the information necessary to rationally form an optimistic attitude about their dispositions. Instead, trust is motivated by a common interest to avoid accidents. Because there is an overlap, or "encapsulation,"[19] of interests, motorists can rationally infer that others will drive responsibly, giving them grounds to entrust them with their safety by sharing the road with them. Understood this way, trust does not appear to be a moral orientation, but a calculated judgment about the interests at play during social interaction. In the ethics literature, this view of trust is called the "epistemological" or "predictive" view of trust.

In response to predictive accounts of trust, advocates for the "moral view" of trust argue that predictive accounts fail to explain the reactive attitudes created by violated trust. If trusting other drivers is simply based on rational inference of a shared interest to avoid accidents, encountering a reckless driver should provoke only surprise that one's assessment of the driver's interests was mistaken; or a judgment that the driver is simply irrational. But encountering a reckless driver produces more than surprise; it produces indignation and blame. So it would seem that viewing trust in light of interest alone does not explain this important element of the common experience of trust. By no means, however, are many of the so-called "moral" accounts of trust immune from this problem. For instance, if trust is grounded on optimism about the other's character, violations of trust should elicit only surprise that the character assessment of the trustee was mistaken. At most, the trustor might express a need to re-evaluate the moral character to the betrayer, but indignation and blame would be misplaced.

Phillip Nickel helpfully observes that both predictive and moral accounts of trust can be consistent with trust as a moral orientation provided one carefully distinguishes (1) trust as a willingness to rely on others while ascribing an obligation to them from (2) the grounds for why one thinks such reliance is warranted.[20] In other words, one should not conflate trust with the inference that the other is trustworthy. The debate between the moral and predictive views about trust can be viewed as a debate about the inference that a trust-candidate is trustworthy. In contrast the reactive moral attitudes created by betrayed trust are based on the ascription of obligation made when one adopts a trust toward a trustee.

With this distinction in place, one can explain the reactive attitudes to betrayed trust while remaining agnostic about the grounds for inferring someone to be trustworthy. One might make such an inference on instrumental grounds, yet still ascribe a moral obligation to the trustee. For instance, drivers on a busy highway assume that others share an interest in avoiding accidents, and this interest assessment serves as a reason to rely on them to drive safely. Such reliance creates a vulnerability that one might believe others have an obligation to respect. Moreover, one might also believe that other drivers have (at least) tacitly agreed to follow the letter and spirit of traffic laws. So while one might view other drivers as being reliable on non-moral grounds (i.e., interest satisfaction), one could still rightfully ascribe a moral obligation to other motorists to drive responsibly. When someone drives recklessly, not only are they judged to be foolish, they are also *blamed* because they create a hazard that violates the agreement to drive within the constraints of the law and fails to respect the vulnerability of other drivers.

The same analysis of trust/trustworthiness can be extended to "moral" accounts of trust as well. When Laura trusted Jeannette to watch her daughter, she did so not only because of common interests, but because she inferred that Jeanette was trustworthy because, as a virtuous friend, she could be relied upon. In extending her vulnerability, she also ascribed an obligation to responsibly care for her daughter.

One need not choose, therefore, between moral and predictive accounts of trust. Both accounts are consistent with the reactive attitudes when trust is betrayed, and both capture important ways in which trust is deemed to be warranted. In many cases, others are judged to be trustworthy because of their moral character, while in other cases trust is warranted in an assessment of overlapping interests. In either case, the reactive attitudes to betrayed trust are explained by the fact that the extension of trust entails an ascription of obligation to the trustee to care responsibly for that which has been entrusted to them.

Bringing these elements together, trust can be defined as an attitude in which there is:

1. a reliance by a trustee
2. on the discretion of another moral agent (i.e., the trustor)
3. in a way that creates vulnerability on the part of the trustor to the discretionary decisions of the trustee
4. warranted by an inference that the other is trustworthy (i.e., will act favorably toward one's interests) because of:

    a. interest alignment between trustor and trustee; or
    b. the character dispositions of the trustor (e.g., beneficence, loyalty)

5. and in light of which the trustor ascribes an obligation to the trustee to care for the trustor's interests:

    a. in light of prior agreement; or
    b. due to the trustor's unique vulnerability to the discretion of the trustee

A trusting relationship is a special, normatively rich one that entails unique obligations to the trusted. Especially when invited, trust can create an obligation on the part of the trustee to responsibly care for the interests entrusted to them. In the context of the professions, invited trust is a functional imperative of professional practice, one that makes professional practice a moral enterprise.

TRUST AND THE PROFESSIONS

Trust is at the heart of the professions. Professional practice is, in essence, an offer of expert assistance, assistance that would be impossible if clients, patients, and the public were unwilling to make themselves vulnerable to individual professionals and self-governing professional communities. For this reason, developing trust is a functional imperative of the professions—they simply could not exist if others were unwilling to entrust important interests to the discretion of professionals. Clients who seek out the expert assistance of a professional, and the public which routinely relies on anonymous professionals and extends varying degrees of self-governance to the professions, create unique vulnerabilities given the important interests at stake and the knowledge and power asymmetries characteristic of the professional relationships. To make such reliance possible, potential clients and the public generally need to see professionals as *worthy* of the trust that they place in them. Given the importance of trust to the very existence of professional practice, there are powerful instrumental, ethical/existential, and moral reasons for professionals, as individual practitioners and members of professional communities, to invite and develop trust from those they intend to serve.

Instrumental Reasons to Invite and Develop Trust

Instrumentally, trust is not only necessary for the very existence of professional practice; it is positively associated with *successful* professional practice. Because reliance on professionals occurs under conditions of risk and knowledge/power asymmetries, without robust levels of trust clients and patients are less likely to seek out the expert assistance of professionals, or when they do, they are more likely to adopt "hedging" strategies aimed at limiting their vulnerability. When hedging, clients and patients fail to share important but sensitive information, or ignore in part or in whole the advice given by the professional. While such hedging strategies can limit the client or patient's vulnerability, they make professional service significantly less effective. For instance, in medicine, patients with higher levels of trust in their physicians are more willing to grant, and rely on, their discretionary power. Such patients are consequently more likely to seek preventative care, are more forthcoming and clear about their conditions, and are more likely to follow through on treatment plans—behaviors that are positively associated with desirable treatment outcomes.[21] Similar patterns are exhibited in law, accounting, financial services, engineering, and a variety of other professions. Trust in professionals supports an increased willingness to rely on them, and this reliance, in turn, enables professionals to better serve clients, patients, and the public.

Trust also has instrumental value to the profession qua profession. One of the hallmarks of the professions is their autonomy, relative to other occupations, in determining the appropriate kinds of education and certification necessary to enter the field. Professional communities play an important gatekeeping function. They also enjoy varying degrees of self-governance in determining the rules of professional conduct and standards of professional practice. The autonomy enjoyed by many of the professions allows them to be self-regulatory and to maintain a certain measure of control over the market of expert services in their field. Indeed, the gatekeeping function in the more formal professions, such as law and medicine, guarantees the professional *monopolization* of important social services. If one wishes to practice law, for instance, licensing requirements necessitate working within the legal profession and satisfying the profession's criteria of entry into the field. This monopolistic control over legal services is designed to guarantee quality professional service by creating high standards of training, ethical conduct,

and mechanisms of accountability. It also, of course, has significant economic value to the members of the profession who are able to eliminate market
competition from agents outside the profession.

Granting the professions such autonomy is a social decision requiring
significant public trust in professionals and in the professional organizations
that exercise self-determination over the profession. When trust in professionals or a professional organization becomes impoverished, the state often
reacts with legal and intrusive means to increasingly regulate, and restrict,
professional practice. Such regulation has a number of negative effects
on professionals. It reduces the autonomy of the professions generally and of
professionals as individual practitioners. Moreover, because legal regulation
is often bureaucratic in nature, it can create inefficiencies for professional
practice. These inefficiencies can be costly and can limit the effectiveness of
the professional service.

Ethical/Existential Reasons to Invite and Develop Trust

Trust is critical to the instrumental success of professional practice and to the
unique social standing of the professions as self-regulating communities.
However, just as love, religious faith, and friendship are not simply strategies
to achieve positive outcomes, the value of trust cannot be accounted for in
purely instrumental terms. Trust has intrinsic value to the quality of the
professional-client relationship, to the professional's sense of virtue, and to
the profession's development as a community. These kinds of reasons are
sometimes understood as "ethical/existential."

Ethical/existential reasons are distinct from instrumental and moral reasons in that they appeal neither to efficiency nor universal obligation. As
opposed to instrumental reasons, which do not assess the value of the ends
being pursued, or moral reasons, which are anchored in the duties incumbent
on all persons, ethical reasons are grounded in the idea of *flourishing* in light
of a consciously pursued way of life.[22] When reasoning ethically, one might
accept that such a way of life is neither a universal duty nor a basic requirement of justice, but is *good* nonetheless because it promotes one's flourishing
as a member of a community collectively pursuing a meaningful goal or
telos. In the context of professional practice, trust is an ethical good because
it promotes the flourishing of both the professional and client.

Trust serves as the emotional core of healthy client-professional relationship and is a basis for the mutual recognition between client and professional
as partners in a joint project. In the trusting professional relationship, the
client *authorizes* the professional to care for an important, entrusted interest
(e.g., health, financial security, liberty). In doing, so the client makes himself
or herself vulnerable to the professional's discretion and ascribes a moral
obligation to the professional to care for his or her vulnerability. The forma-

tion of the caring relationship promotes an emotional richness to professional practice that makes the experience more meaningful and rewarding for both client and professional. When caring, the professional adopts an attitude of concern about those they serve and promotes their relevant interests not simply because "the job" requires it, but because it expresses the professional's responsiveness to the unique vulnerability of those they serve. In a trust-based professional practice, the client and professional transcend their status as economic agents and create a shared project of care. This makes professional relationships different from mere agency relationships in which an agent simply carries out the will of a client or customer. Even in such thin relationships, there is an important element of trust. However, professional relationships are much richer than this in that expert assistance is being offered to the client in an effort to care for, or promote, specific interests that the client cannot care for him or herself. While clients may in some cases choose to grant to the professional the lion's share of the decision making, professional relationships are typically collaborations on the part of client and professional in providing care for the client's interests.

For professionals, inviting and earning client trust promotes a form of personal and professional excellence or virtue. Alasdair MacIntyre defines virtue as:

> An acquired human quality the possession and exercise of which tends to enable us to achieve those goods which are internal to practices and the lack of which effectively prevents us from achieving any such goods.[23]

The disposition to invite, develop, and honor trust promotes the achievement of the essential or internal goods of professional practice. The telos of profession practice is to provide expert assistance to persons in need: in law, to promote procedural justice; in medicine, to promote health and alleviate suffering; and, in engineering, to promote efficient and safe design. Things such as health, justice, and safety are the internal goods of those practices, goods better achieved by professionals disposed to invite, develop, and honor the trust of those they seek to assist. Those who consciously pursue the telos of their profession and think it important have good reasons to engage in practices that promote the effective fulfillment of that telos. In other words, to take seriously one's professional practice is to value doing that activity *well.*

Like the development of technical skill, which is another virtue of professional practice, the development of one's trustworthiness and one's disposition to form trusting relationships with clients is also an important means of individual flourishing of a professional. Understood in the context of the professional telos, such flourishing is intrinsically valuable.

Flourishing also has value for professionals as an important source of self-esteem and a sense of fulfillment through one's work. *Good* professionals, those who take seriously the goal of providing expert assistance to clients, take pride in their ability to develop and earn the trust of their clients and are gratified by successfully caring for their client's interests. In engineering, Samuel Forman calls this the "existential pleasure"[24] that comes from doing one's work well. Any virtuous professional feels pleasure from doing his or her work well, but this is especially true in the so-called "helping" professions. For professions that are poorly compensated financially (e.g., education, social work, counseling), the joy that comes from successfully helping students, clients, and patients is often, quite frankly, the *primary* reward for one's professional work.

The professional's sense of flourishing and the meaningfulness of his or her work are also promoted by the prestige of the profession, prestige intrinsically tied to the trustworthiness of professionals and professional communities. Nurses, for instance, are routinely ranked among the most trustworthy of professionals, a fact that they point to with pride.

The flourishing promoted by inviting, earning, and honoring trust is by no means strictly individualistic. Developing trustworthiness as a virtue also serves as a basis for the mutual recognition of fellow professionals as members of an *ethical community*. From a technical standpoint, professional communities create and maintain discourses on a range of issues such as the nature of proper training for professional, proper credentialing, developments in the latest practices, techniques, and technologies. These discourses, supported by professional associations and institutions, are the basis by which professionals recognize one another as members of an expert community. However, what is most distinctive about the professions is not their expertise, for there are many occupations that require expertise yet do not rise to the level of a profession, but rather their participation in an institutionalized ethical discourse that addresses the nature of professional responsibility and sets rigorous ethical standards concretized in codes of ethics, oaths, ethics education, and ethical requirements for credentialing. By engaging in the intersubjective project of being worthy of client and public trust, professionals transcend their status as individuals and become partners in an intergenerational communal project oriented toward the realization of the professional telos.

Moral Reasons to Develop Trust

Finally, professionals have good *moral* reasons to invite and develop trust from those whom they serve. At the heart of moral accountability is the "second-person standpoint"—a participatory stance by which one engages the Other in a will-to-will, or "I-Thou," relationship and recognizes him or her as a free and equal member of the moral community. In the professions, the development of the fiduciary relationship between professional and client is an *intersubjective accomplishment* that allows the client-professional relationship to transcend the one-dimensionality of economic exchange and become richly moral—an "I-Thou" relationship by which client and professional mutually recognize one another as *persons*.[25] For clients, the recognition of their personhood plays an important role in supporting and promoting their right to autonomy. This is especially true when clients interact with professionals while in extreme states of vulnerability. When professionals invite and work to earn the trust of clients, they recognize the client as a person in a caring I-Thou relationship. Such a relationship can be an important foundation that bolsters the existential security the client needs to exercise his or her right to autonomous decision making.

The obligation to invite and develop client and public trust is also a requirement of reciprocal justice, particularly in the principle "fair play" developed by H. L .A. Hart[26] and John Rawls.[27] When engaged in cooperative activity, agents rightfully ascribe to others an obligation to do their fair share to make the activity successful. When agents benefit from engaging in cooperative behavior, but fail to do their fair share, other participants experience reactive attitudes such as blame, resentment, and moral indignation. This occurs for instance in the well-known "free rider" scenario. Suppose a group meets weekly and each member contributes a small amount of money for the purpose of providing pizza. When a particular member of the group, Joe, comes and helps himself to the pizza, but consistently does not contribute, he "free rides" on the cooperative activity.

Free riding is wrong because it violates the moral obligation of "fair play." Rawls argues that when (1) there exists a mutually beneficial cooperative scheme, (2) that is otherwise just, and (3) an individual *voluntarily* helps him or herself to the scheme's benefits, then there is an obligation, as a matter of justice, to follow through on the expectations that the scheme places on each beneficiary.[28] In the pizza case, there is a mutually beneficial scheme in which everyone in the group gets pizza. Joe knowingly and voluntarily helps himself to the benefits of that scheme. As a matter of fairness he has an obligation to do his fair share to promote the scheme, because each person benefits by having pizza at the group meeting. The fair burden for each member is to contribute for the purchase of the pizza.

The obligation to fair play can be justified from a variety of perspectives. For Rawls, parties in the original position have good reason to choose such a principle because without it, many cooperative schemes would become impossible. This would severely limit the availability of primary social goods. As such, from an impartial perspective there are good reasons to demand that all individuals abide by the principle of fair play. Moreover, free riders take advantage of others who contribute fairly to the cooperative scheme—a form of exploitation for which rational persons would reasonably refuse to grant permission. As free and equal members of the moral community, agents deserve respect for the contributions they make to mutually beneficial cooperative schemes. The free rider denies that respect and *exploits* those efforts. Because there is a basic right to be free from exploitation—a right that can be justified from most normative perspectives—free riding is prohibited as a matter of justice.

A profession is a cooperative scheme. Professions are unique social arrangements in which society bestows privileged legal and cultural status to certain occupational groups. Professional communities typically enjoy significant degrees of cultural capital, community self-regulation, and workplace autonomy relative to other occupations. The "gate keeping" function of the more formal professions creates a social arrangement in which the profession enjoys a self-governing monopoly over important social services. This monopoly often has significant financial benefits for members of the profession. Moreover, the professions are also accorded significant prestige, which translates into various forms of social capital.

In return for supporting the existence of the professions, the public expects professionals who are well trained and able to provide expert assistance. Successfully providing such assistance requires professionals to develop trust with clients, and the public generally. Without trust, clients do not seek out professional assistance, or when they do, that assistance is not nearly as effective as it could, and should, be. Professionals who do not invite and develop trust, or who act in ways that undermine that trust, fail to live up to their end of the social bargain and consequently take advantage of those who contribute their fair share to the professions as a social arrangement. Becoming a professional is a voluntary choice, one that brings with it significant benefits. Professionals know this and voluntarily help themselves to the benefits of their status.

Having helped themselves to the considerable benefits of being a professional, they now have an obligation to do their part to promote effective expert assistance—assistance that requires the development of client and public trust. Those who fail to do so free ride, or exploit, their professional role. As Andrew Brien puts it, adopting a professional role is "an implicit promise to use one's capacities altruistically," a promise that can only be fulfilled when those who rely on professionals trust them. "As the professional has promised to help, it follows that the professional has an obligation to do those things that will lead to the client being helped."[29]

TRUST IN THE PROFESSIONAL ROLE

The instrumental, ethical, and moral reasons to invite and develop trust apply to professionals not only as individual practitioners, but as members of professional communities as well. This is because in modern societies, clients and the public often interact with professionals under relatively anonymous conditions. Gone are the days of the family doctor or lawyer. As previously noted, clients typically interact with professionals while having little, if any, personal familiarity with them. Many interactions with professionals are also not iterative. A patient who sees a doctor at an urgent care clinic may well have never met the doctor before, and may never do so again. For its part, the public relies on professionals whom they will never meet. From the perspective of trust, such conditions are "thin," in that they do not provide the kind of familiarity needed for trust evaluators to infer that trust-candidates are reliable. How can professionals invite and develop robust levels of *anonymous trust* under such impersonal and anonymous conditions?

Anonymous trust can be created by the development of trusted social *roles*. A social role is a set of practices, rights, and expectations that locate an agent in a particular position within a social network.[30] A social role is a particular, and to some degree, culturally standardized, "part" that one plays in concerted social action. As such, roles are identifiable positions in interactive social networks that are "scripted," in that the occupation of a role comes with the expectation of a variety of interconnected performances.

Professional roles are interesting in a number of respects. They are voluntary social roles constructed by the community of role-players themselves. Because of the autonomy and self-regulation enjoyed by many professions, professional communities play an essential role in defining the rights, expectations, and best practices of professional role-players. From the standpoint of technical expertise, this is accomplished by setting standards of education and practical proficiency. A professional community can then use its "credentialing" function to create a "reputation" for those who are certified by the community to occupy the professional role. Accordingly, a client or member of the public will have a variety of expectations about, for instance, the skill of an accountant because that accountant has been credentialed by the accounting community and is thus a bona fide role-player. Without even knowing the accountant personally, one can have confidence in the accountant's expertise because of the quality control function of the professional community.

A similar process takes place in terms of trust. In thin social conditions, clients and members of the public do not have enough information to rationally develop the robust levels of trust necessary to enter the kinds of fiduciary relationships essential to professional practice. Here, the reputation of the social role can fill in the gaps and allow trust to be developed between client and professional, even in the absence of personal familiarity. In many cases, clients are ready to extend prima facie trust to the professional before he or she even walks into the room because they are bona fide members of the professional community. Likewise, professional reputation provides reason for the public to extend unique authority to professionals and the professions themselves.

Just as in expectations about expertise, the professional community primes the expectations of the general public regarding the trustworthiness of those who occupy the professional role. For this reason, professional communities go to great lengths to assure the public that those who occupy professional roles will conduct themselves in a manner worthy of client and public trust. The institutionalization of the professional role through mission statements, codes of ethics, and the public activity of professional organizations can build a fund of trusting expectations on the part of clients. Individual professionals can then capitalize on this fund of trusting expectations to build anonymous trust with clients and members of the public.

The work of the profession as an ethical community will be discussed at greater length in chapter 4. The point here is that because professionals typically interact with clients and the public in relatively anonymous and impersonal social situations, they rely heavily on the development of a trusted professional role to create the trust necessary on the part of clients if they are to rely on the professional. Because of this, the reasons that professionals have to invite and develop trust apply not only to their practice with clients, but by extension, to professional communities. As members of professional communities, professionals have instrumental ethical, and moral reasons to promote standards of ethical conduct, and regimes of ethical education and compliance, that promote the trusting expectations on the part of the general public. Doing so has instrumental, ethical/existential, and moral value.

CONCLUSION

In its essence, professional practice is an offer of expert assistance in which the professional invites a client to entrust valuable interests to his or her care. The professional-client relationship then is, broadly speaking, a fiduciary one. But because entering such a relationship entails risk under conditions of uncertainty, professional practice requires the development of trust of those they serve.

Trust is necessary for reliable professional practice. Indeed, if levels of trust are sufficiently impoverished, clients will not seek out the expert assistance of the professional at all. Because of this, professionals have a variety of reasons to invite and earn the trust of clients. For individual practitioners, client trust makes their practice more effective and promotes the prestige of their social position. It also enriches their relationship with clients and their fellow professionals. Finally, inviting and developing trust lives up to the expectations of the mutually beneficial cooperative scheme that socially supports the professions.

Because professionals typically interact with clients under relatively thin conditions, they rely on the perceived trustworthiness of their professional role. The instrumental, ethical, and moral reasons for developing trust with clients, by extension, also apply to the work of the professional as members of the professional communities. Professionals have good reasons, indeed a moral obligation, to work within their professional organizations and institutions to develop rules of conduct for all who occupy the professional role that promote trust in the occupiers of that role.

The development of client trust therefore cannot be done by a professional alone, but requires the intersubjective work of a community engaged in a variety of discourses about the proper nature of the professional role and how the public can best be assured of the professional's trustworthiness. The professional community is best positioned to provide such assurance by clearly identifying the nature of trustworthiness as understood in light of the community telos. By understanding the nature of "the trustworthy professional," professional communities can promote reliability in practitioners and a reputation for trustworthiness in the professional role.

NOTES

1. For instance, see Michael Bayles, *Professional Ethics*, 2nd ed. (Belmont CA: Wadsworth 1989). See also, Paul Faber, "Client and Professional," in *Ethics for the Professions*, ed. John Rowan and Samuel Zinaich, Jr. (Belmont, CA: Wadsworth, 2003): 125–34.

2. E.C. Hui, "Doctors as Fiduciaries: A Legal Construct of the Patient-Physician Relationship," *Hong Kong Journal of Medicine* 11, no. 6 (2005): 527–29.

3. Max Weber, *Economy and Society*, trans. and ed. Guenther Roth, Claus Wittich, (Los Angeles: University of California Press: 1968), 956–58.

4. Jürgen Habermas, *Between Facts and Norms*, trans. William Regh (Cambridge, MA: MIT Press, 1998), 486.

5. Annette Baier, "Trust and Anti-Trust," *Ethics* 96, no. 2 (1986); Russell Hardin, "Conceptions and Explanations of Trust," in *Trust in Society*, ed. Karen Cook (New York: Russell Sage Foundation, 2001).

6. Harold Garfinkel, "Studies in the Routine Grounds of Everyday Activities," in *Studies in Ethnomethodology* (Englewood Cliffs, NJ: Prentice Hall, 1967), 71.

7. Harold Garfinkel, "A Conception of, and Experiments with 'Trust' as a Condition of Stable Concerted Action," in *Motivation and Social Interaction*, ed. O.J. Harvey (New York: Ronald Press, 1963), 199.

8. Baier, "Trust and Anti-Trust," 235.

9. Marc A. Cohen and John Dienhart, "Moral and Amoral Conceptions of Trust, with an Application in Organizational Ethics," *Journal of Business Ethics* 112 (2013): 9.

10. Philip Nickel, "Trust and Obligation-Ascription," *Ethical Theory and Moral Practice* 10 (2007): 309–19. See also, Baier, "Trust and Anti-Trust," 236.

11. See David Hume, *A Treatise on Human Nature* (Oxford: Clarendon Press, 1967 [1739]). John Stuart Mill, *Utilitarianism* (New York: Hackett Publishing, 2002).

12. Robert Goodin, *Protecting the Vulnerable* (Chicago: University of Chicago Press, 1985), 34.

13. Baier, "Trust and Anti-Trust," 251. See also, Goodin, 70–92.

14. Baier, "Trust and Anti-Trust," 240.

15. For an account of attitude vs. grounds for trust see, Nickel, 312–13.

16. Baier, "Trust and Antitrust," 231–60. Baier, "Trust and its Vulnerabilities," *The Tanner Lectures on Human Values* vol. 13 (Salt Lake City: University of Utah Press, 1992).

17. Russell Hardin, "The Street-Level Epistemology of Trust," *Politics and Society* 21 (1993): 505–29.

18. Russell Hardin, "Conceptions and Explanations of Trust," in *Trust in Society,* ed. Karen Cook (New York: Russell Sage Foundation, 2001), 7.

19. Hardin, "Conceptions and Explanations of Trust," 3.

20. Nickel, "Trust as Obligation-Ascription," 314. See also Cohen and Dienhart, "Moral and Amoral Conceptions of Trust."

21. Mark Hall, Elizabeth Dugan, Beiyao Zheng, and Aneil Mishra, "Trust in Physicians and Medical Institutions: What Is It? Can It Be Measured? and Does It Matter?" *Milbank Quarterly* 79, no. 4 (2001): 613–39.

22. Jürgen Habermas, "On the Employment of Practical Reason," in *Justification and Application*, trans. and ed. Ciaran Cronen (Cambridge, MA: MIT Press, 1993).

23. Alasdair MacIntyre, *After Virtue* (South Bend, IN: Notre Dame University Press), 178.

24. Samuel C. Florman, *The Existential Pleasures of Engineering*, 2nd ed. (New York: St. Martin's Griffin, 1994).

25. Edmund Pellegrino and David Thomasma, *The Virtues in Medical Practice* (New York: Oxford University Press, 1993).

26. H. L. A. Hart, "Are There any Natural Rights?" *Philosophical Review* 64, no. 2 (1955): 175–91.

27. John Rawls, *A Theory of Justice: Revised Edition* (Cambridge, MA: Belknap Press, 1999): 93–98.

28. Ibid.

29. Andrew Brien, "Professional Ethics and the Culture of Trust," *Journal of Business Ethics* 17, no. 4 (1998): 403.

30. Judith Andre, "Role Morality as a Complex Instance of Ordinary Morality," *American Philosophical Quarterly* 28, no.1 (1991): 73.

Chapter Three

The Trustworthy Professional

Professionals have instrumental, ethical, and moral reasons to invite and develop the trust of those they intend to serve. The warrant for trust is the inference that the trustee possesses properties that make it likely that he or she will responsibly care for interests entrusted to them—that is, they are *trustworthy*. Because the inference of trustworthiness is essential to developing trust, professionals have good reasons to develop *effective trustworthiness*. Being effectively trustworthy entails (1) being trustworthy—that is, being the kind of person in whom one can rationally entrust with the care of interests, and (2) effectively signaling this trustworthiness to others.[1] Trustworthiness without effective signaling will not promote trust because agents rely on such signals when inferring the trustworthiness of trust-candidates. Conversely, effective signaling of one's trustworthiness without actually being trustworthy amounts to immoral deception.

The literature on trustworthiness can be grouped into instrumental and dispositional schools of thought. "Instrumental" accounts of trustworthiness define agents as trustworthy when their interests are such that they can be rationally relied upon to respond favorably to the interests entrusted to them. Advocates of "dispositional" approaches, on the other hand, argue that agents are only trustworthy when they have a disposition to take the trustor's dependence as a reason to care for the interests entrusted to them. Instrumental accounts of trustworthiness provide an important resource for professionals when developing anonymous trust with clients and the public. However, in the context of the professions, instrumental trustworthiness alone is insufficient to protect the vulnerability of those relying on professionals. Trustworthy professionals reliably care for those who depend on them, even when it is not in their interest to do so. This requires that professionals be dispositionally trustworthy via the possession of a variety of character virtues.

INSTRUMENTAL TRUSTWORTHINESS

When the traffic light turns green and a driver edges her car out into the intersection, she trusts that those drivers facing red lights will stop. If mistaken, she could be badly injured or even killed. Great trust is placed in other drivers even though one knows nothing about their character. In such cases, trust is based on the inference that there is a shared interest among drivers to avoid accidents. Traffic accidents are dangerous and expensive for all involved, so any driver can reasonably predict that other drivers will act in ways to avoid them. Having such a shared interest makes other drivers trustworthy relative to the avoidance of accidents.

For some ethicists and social scientists, this confluence of interest is the essence of being trustworthy. Recall that trust is "three part" involving a trustee, a trustor, and a particular action ϕ or action domain. From the instrumental perspective, a trustee is *trustworthy* if (1) relative to the trustor, and (2) regarding ϕ or in the ϕ action domain, (3) it is in the trustee's interests to responsibly care for that entrusted to him or her by the trustor. Russell Hardin, perhaps the leading advocate for this approach, illustrates this nicely with a story from Dostoyevsky's *The Brothers Karamazov*.[2] Dmitry Karamazov tells a parable involving a lieutenant colonel responsible for a significant financial account with the army. After audits are completed on his books, he takes available funds that would have sat dormant and lends them to a "trustworthy" local merchant named Trifonov, who uses them in a profitable business. Trifonov then returns the money with interest and a gift. This mutually beneficial arrangement is illegal, so the lieutenant colonel must trust that Trifonov will return the money—which he does because it is in his interests to preserve his beneficial relationship with the lieutenant colonel. One day, however, a new commander demands an account of the unit's finances. The lieutenant colonel rushes to Trifonov and asks him to return the money he recently gave him, to whom Trifonov responds, "I've never received any money from you, and could not possibly have received any."[3] Because the arrangement is illegal, the lieutenant colonel can do little about Trifonov's betrayal. After a failed suicide attempt, he is forced to retire from the Army in disgrace.

Hardin, like Dmitry Karamazov, uses this parable to illustrate the point that trustworthiness is a matter of "encapsulated interest."[4] Trifonov was trustworthy only to the point that preserving his relationship with the lieutenant colonel was in his interest. His interest in securing future loans from the officer gave him an incentive not to defect and betray the officer's trust, but once that interest was removed, Trifonov was no longer trustworthy. Had their arrangement been legal, Trifonov's self-interest would have been augmented with a series of external inducements to be reliable. If legal, the officer could have appealed to contract law, social shaming, and other institutional and social constraints. Without recourse to such constraints, the officer was forced to trust Trifonov only on the basis of the mutually beneficial nature of their enterprise, and once this benefit evaporated, so did Trifonov's trustworthiness.

In the professional context, this kind of trustworthiness is grounded in the aligned interests between client and professional. These interests both are internal to the relationship and come from external constraints. When a patient visits a doctor, it is perhaps natural to think that their interests are aligned. The patient wishes to be healed, and the doctor has an interest in healing the patient—after all, physicians choose this line of work because of their desire to be healers. Moreover, the patient can take into account the institutional constraints on the physician in the form of legal and professional disincentives for misconduct. Malpractice litigation and the potential loss of one's license to practice medicine create incentives for the doctor to provide adequate care. Finally, it is good for the doctor's business to provide high quality service. One might conclude that the physician's interest in preserving the relationship with his or her patient brings the patient's and physician's interest into harmony or, as Hardin puts it, the patient's interest is "encapsulated" within the physician's. As the physician egoistically promotes his or her own interest, he or she takes on the interests of the patient.

But beneath the surface there is also significant *misalignment* of the interests between patient and physician. Physicians working in managed care environments typically have various incentives to treat patients quickly or to recommend expensive procedures even if they are not necessary or only marginally so. Moreover, many patient-physician interactions are "one-off" interactions, as when a patient seeks the assistance of a surgeon. Without an enduring relationship to consider, the possibility of self-interested betrayal on the part of the physician increases.[5] Even aside from conflicts of interest, medical decisions are not simply technical, but routinely involve values that the physician does not necessarily share with the patient. For instance, as healers, physicians tend to favor treatments that prolong life even when patients do not prefer it. Physicians also tend to favor their field of expertise when proposing treatment plans. So the physician may have multiple reasons not to take on the interests of the patient.

Recourse to institutional constraints, such as legal mechanisms, should not provide much comfort here either. While it true that such constraints provide incentives for physicians to avoid the most egregious forms of misconduct, litigation and enforcement of institutional (including legal) regulations are notoriously ineffective and expensive. Malpractice litigation is very expensive and time consuming, creating numerous transaction costs for the patient. Furthermore, given the knowledge asymmetries rife in patient-physician relationships, patients are often in a poor position to determine if a negative outcome occurred because of professional misconduct.

As the Trifonov story itself indicates, trustworthiness grounded in interest encapsulation can be fundamentally unstable as shifts in interests can lead to betrayal on the part of the trustee.[6] As some critics point out, instrumental trustworthiness can be unstable even if interests remain stable. For instance, if Trifinov becomes satisfied with the monies he has made via his arrangement with the officer, he may at any time rationally choose to "defect" from their arrangement. His trustworthiness depends not only on his interests, but also his desire to maximize them. Shifting strategies—from maximizing to satisficing for instance—can also make one instrumentally untrustworthy.[7]

Given that many client-professional interactions are noniterative; that they entail significant knowledge asymmetries and a certain measure of unavoidable conflict of interest; and that appeal to external constraints such as litigation create high transaction costs, trustworthiness as encapsulated interest alone will not serve as an adequate basis for the professional's trustworthiness. Trust based on interest alignment alone would be impoverished and rife with "hedging" strategies that would make professional practice significantly less effective. What is necessary is that professionals be trustworthy even when it is not in their immediate self-interest. This stronger sense of trustworthiness is rooted not in one's interests, but in one's character.

DISPOSITIONAL TRUSTWORTHINESS

Fortunately for professionals and those they serve, interest encapsulation is not the only warrant for inferring trustworthiness. Such an inference can also be developed by appeals to the dispositional character traits of the trust-candidate. Karen Jones, for instance, has developed an attractive account of trustworthiness focused on the idea of *conscientiousness*, which is a disposition to take the trusting reliance of others as a reason to care for the interests one has been entrusted with.[8] In her view, someone is *trustworthy* when:

1. relative to the trustor
2. relative to a particular action or action domain
3. the trustor's vulnerable dependence on the trustee counts as a "compelling reason"[9] for the trustee to responsibly care for the interests entrusted by the trustor
4. the trustee has character traits or dispositions such that this reason is effective in motivating action; and
5. the trustee is competent to care for the entrusted interest

Dispositional trustworthiness does not require that the trustor judge the trustee to be trustworthy in all respects or in all action domains. There are few if any persons who meet the criteria of trustworthiness in all domains because, at the very least, few, if any, individuals possess reliable competence in all action-domains. Because trust is relative to specific actions or action-domains, it is possible for relatively immoral agents to judge one another as dispositionally trustworthy. For instance, a criminal gang member might infer a peer's trustworthiness in light of his or her dispositional *loyalty to the gang.*

The key intuition at work in the idea of dispositional trustworthiness is captured in condition number 3. Someone is trustworthy when the dependence and vulnerability of the trustee counts as a compelling reason for them to responsibly care for the entrusted interest. It is for this reason that most people intuitively think of Trifonov as untrustworthy, even while he was still cooperating with the army officer. His reliability was fundamentally unstable because it was grounded only in a contingent confluence of interests between himself and the officer. On the dispositional account, to be trustworthy, Trifonov would need to take the lieutenant colonel's dependence on him as a compelling reason to be reliable. Because Trifonov did not do so, he was untrustworthy in the dispositional sense.

Those who are trustworthy in the dispositional sense take the dependence of the trustor as a compelling reason to be reliable. To call this reason "compelling" does not imply that it absolutely binding. A compelling reason is one that, as Jones puts it, "is not an overriding one, but it is not easily outweighed."[10] A compelling reason is ranked higher relative to other reasons, and is set aside only in special circumstances where other compelling reasons are at play. Because trust, as described in the last chapter, involves an ascription of an obligation to the trustee, someone is trustworthy when he or she is the kind of person who *recognizes*, when appropriate, the ascribed obligation as a compelling reason to responsibly care for the entrusted interests.

When someone is trustworthy, they not only recognize the trustor's dependence as a compelling reason for action, but also have a disposition to be motivated to action by that reason. This makes the reason "internal" in that it is one recognized by the trustee as a reason *for him or her* in a motivationally efficacious manner.[11] While there are a variety of accounts of how reasons become consistently efficacious, there is a long and rich tradition that explains this efficaciousness of reasons through character development.

The Greek term "character" originally meant a distinctive mark or stamp on a coin. The Ancient Greek philosophers adopted the idea of such a distinctive and rather permanent mark as a way to explain how agents could reliably act for the good—an essential element for living a flourishing life. For Plato and Aristotle, the reliability of acting well requires the proper relationship between one's cognitive and affective capabilities. Plato dramatically illustrates this in *The Phaedrus* with his metaphor of the charioteer whose capacity to steer is significantly dependent on the training of the horses with which he works. Plato asks his reader to imagine a charioteer with two horses, one black and one white. The black horse represents the appetites while the white horse represents the nonappetitive affective states (e.g., pride, anger, shame). Guiding the chariot well routinely requires the charioteer to steer in directions not preferred by the black horse. This is because appetitive states steer one toward short-term satisfaction at the expense of both long-term appetite satisfaction and other valuable goods that make up a flourishing life. Acting well requires agents to control and redirect the appetites. This is easier said than done because the black horse is far stronger than the charioteer, whose tug on the rein is hardly noticed by the raging power of the appetites. For the charioteer to have effective and reliable control, he or she will need the white horse to be responsive to commands. This, in turn, will only be possible if the white horse is properly trained to respond appropriately to the charioteer's input. In other words, only if the nonappetitive affective states (e.g., pride, shame, indignation) are properly trained to support practical wisdom can agents reliably act for the good. The good training of the white horse represents the virtuous character of an agent. When their character is properly developed, agents have the right kinds of feelings for the right kinds of things.

CHARACTER, VIRTUE, AND TRUSTWORTHINESS

Character is a stable set of personality traits (e.g., attitudes and emotions) that motivationally link the insights of practical reasoning with action. When those personality traits support the insights of practical reasoning, they can be described as *virtues*. A virtue is an integration or harmony between practical insight and efficacious motivations—or as Rosalind Hursthouse puts it, a virtue is a character trait that "goes all the way down" and links "emotions and emotional reactions, choices, values, desires, perceptions, attitudes, interests, expectations and sensibilities. To possess a virtue is to be a certain sort of person with a certain complex mindset."[12] This mindset provides motivational support for one's rational deliberation into what is required to act well.

But what does it mean to "act well"? Alasdair MacIntyre argues that an individual acts well when promoting the achievement of the essential, or intrinsic, goods of his or her practice.[13] Thus a virtue is a set of personality traits that consistently link one's insight into acting well and one's motivation to follow through on that insight. Someone who is honest, for instance, consistently experiences positive feelings (e.g., enjoyment, pride) at the prospect or accomplishment of truthful communication *in the right circum-*

stances. Those who are honest promote the achievement of the intrinsic good of communication—the symbolically mediated sharing of information.

Possessing character traits that support the insights of practical delibera-tion is essential for ethical action for a number of reasons, not the least of which is the problem of what the Ancient Greeks called *akrasia*—a weakness of will in which an agent identifies the correct course of action through practical deliberation, but fails to act rightly because he or she is motivated by inappropriate feelings, such as short-term appetite satisfaction. Take a trivial example. Suppose Robert recognizes that an important part of human flourishing is maintaining a proper diet, and his doctor has advised him to lose some weight. As a result he tries to make health-conscious menu deci-sions while he shops. Suppose that as he comes to the ice cream aisle he sees a large display of his favorite ice cream, and now, as if "drunk" (as Aristotle thinks of it), his motivational support for his reason to avoid ice cream dissolves and he comes to take his short-term appetite satisfaction as an effective reason for action. After buying and eating the ice cream, Robert recalls that he had good reasons to avoid doing so and reproaches himself for his weakness of will—his character was not sufficiently strong enough to make good reasons to avoid ice cream *effective* ones and he thus suffered *akrasia*. The development of the one's character strengthens one's ability to consistently and firmly act in ways that promote the insights of practical deliberation.

The Situationist Challenge

While the idea that agents can have stable dispositions is widely assumed in folk psychology, and is generally considered a key element in forming (or withholding) trust, critics such as John Dorris[14] and Gilbert Harman[15] argue that there is much empirical research demonstrating that individuals do not have such traits. For instance, in the famous "Good Samaritan" experiment, a number of Princeton Theological Seminary students were told they needed to record a lecture in another building on campus. Some were told that they were running late and needed to hurry because the assistant conducting the recording was already waiting for them; some were told they would be on time if they left immediately; and some were told they would be a few minutes early for the recording session. As the students left the building they encountered a man slumped on the steps who coughed twice and groaned as they walked past. The "hurry" students were the least likely to stop and offer to help the man. The "early" students were the most likely to help.[16]

The lesson that *situationists* such as Dorris and Harman draw from this experiment is that character traits, such as beneficence or empathy, do not guide behavior; rather features of an action-situation drive behavior. Presum-ing the students had more or less the same character disposition of beneficence, the key to whether they stopped to help the sick man had little to do with their character and much to do with the situation—whether they were in a hurry was decisive, not their beneficence. Situationists conclude that the idea of character virtue is incoherent. If individuals do not have something like stable, enduring character dispositions, then they cannot have virtues—and because "ought implies can"—there can be no obligation to develop virtues that do not exist.

The situationist challenge is a serious one. Without stable dispositions, dispositional trustworthiness would be impossible.[17] This would leave individuals with only instrumental trust, which is too riddled with hedging strategies to form the trust for effective professional practice. But does the empirical research really show there are no dispositional states such as character virtues? Certainly, it shows a particularly flatfooted version of virtue does not exist. Sometimes virtues are understood as thoughtless habits by which persons reflexively act in a predictable manner across time and action contexts. An honest person, it is supposed, communicates truthfully "without a second thought" because they have been habituated to do so. Virtues, construed this way, are "behavioral" dispositions.

Empirical research such as the "Good Samaritan" experiment indicates that there are good reasons to doubt the existence of character virtues understood as thoughtless habits. However, it is important to emphasize that virtues are not habits, but are personality structures which link rational insight with motivation. A person possessing the virtue of honesty is motivationally responsive to certain kinds of reasons for acting. "It would be a lie," counts as a powerful reason not to act for the honest individual. Because virtues link motivation and reason, how a virtuous person behaves in any given situation will be matter of a *principled* dispositional response to the reasons at play in any given situation. In many situations, there are a variety of goods at stake, and the virtuous individual must weigh the different reasons for acting, make the appropriate judgment, and then act.

Consider again the "Good Samaritan" experiment. The students who were rushed (the "hurry" students), it could be argued, weighed the importance of their punctuality versus the needs of the distressed man. They decided, rightly or wrongly, that their punctuality was more important, and motivated by conscientiousness for those waiting for them, they decided to pass by the distressed man. On this explanation, the different responses to the sick man can be interpreted as responses to the conflicting reasons for action, and hence different virtues that are at play, rather than a lack of character dispositions altogether.

The idea that the "Good Samaritan" experiment is really about a "conflict of reasons" rather than a lack of character is supported by a replication of experiment conducted several years later. In this later iteration, some of the "hurry" students were *also* told their task was unimportant. The result?

Whereas only 10 percent of the "hurry" student stopped to help the man in the first experiment, 70 percent of the "hurry/low importance" students stopped to help in the second.[18] What was decisive was not the morally irrelevant features of the situation, but judgments made by the students as to what was most important in the given situation—beneficence or conscientiousness. Their character dispositions then motivated them to act on that decision.[19]

Of course, the "hurry" students in the first experiment may have made the wrong decision, but whether they did so or not is an issue of moral reasoning, not evidence that character virtues do not exist. Indeed, much of this literature points to the conclusion reached by Thomas Aquinas—that prudence is a cardinal virtue because the exercise of the virtues generally depends on making good judgments.

THE VIRTUES OF THE TRUSTWORTHY PROFESSIONAL

The situationist challenge helps clarify the idea of virtue as a principled disposition by which the individual is motivationally responsive to certain kinds of reasons. Because professionals invite and develop trust with clients, patients, employers, and members of the public, they have good reasons to develop the character virtues that will make them worthy of that trust. Possessing a trustworthy character promotes their reliable care of the interests entrusted to them by clients, patients, and the general public. In turn, being reliable—and effectively signaling that reliability—promotes the development of trust. Given the unique nature of the professional relationships, the trustworthy professional needs to possess a variety of character virtues such as loyalty, honesty, and beneficence.

The dispositions that make a professional trustworthy can be thought of as virtues from both an internal and external perspective. Internally, virtues can be defined, as Macintyre does, as traits necessary for the achievement of the internal goods of a particular practice. The character traits that make professionals trustworthy are important to developing trusting relationships that, in turn, are necessary for the achievement of the internal goods of professional practice. More broadly, virtue is defined, as it is by Plato and Aristotle, as those traits that promote human flourishing itself. Even understood this way, the character traits that make professionals trustworthy can be understood as virtues because the goods serviced by professionals—justice, health, safety, financial security—are rightly thought of as key elements in human flourishing. Moreover, in democratic societies, the professions are generally just institutions in that membership is open to all members of the community, service is provided on a nondiscriminatory basis, and the professions generally promote the rights of individuals. So, from both an internal and external perspective, the character traits that make professions trustworthy are reasonably thought of as virtues.

Given the unique nature of the professional practice as an offer of expert assistance and the fiduciary nature of most client-professional relationships, the development of those virtues that make professionals trustworthy is not optional, but is obligatory for all who wish to be professionals. This is also true for those professionals who do not serve specific clients. Judges, prosecutors, public engineers, and public administrators might not enter direct fiduciary relationships with clients, but they nonetheless invite public trust and enjoy the power and privileges that are the fruit of that trust. Such professionals can be reasonably said to be in an *indirect fiduciary relationship* with the public. The public authorizes such professionals to care for important public interests such as justice, safety, and efficiency of social systems on the basis that these professionals, and their professions, present themselves as trustworthy caretakers of the public interest. Even professionals in the private sector invite, and accept, public trust to care for important public interests. For this reason, engineers in the private sector have a duty to promote public safety. Given these duties, trustworthy professionals develop the virtues that make them responsive to the vulnerability of those they serve, whether specific clients or the broader public.

Much ink has been spilled of late in professional ethics literature as to whether professional ethics should be thought of in terms of duties (as deontologists and utilitarians have tended to argue) or virtues (as virtue theorists have argued). From the standpoint of trust, however, duty, and virtue work dialectically. Professionals have an obligation to invite, develop and honor trust with those they wish to serve, and this requires the development of the virtues necessary to become trustworthy professionals.

In the domain of professional practice, there is wide agreement as to the basic contours of the obligations created by the professional fiduciary relationship: loyalty, beneficence, respect for autonomy, honesty, discretion, and diligence. Michael Bayles refers to these as the "obligations of trustworthiness."[20] Trustworthy professionals have principled dispositions to act in ways that honor these obligations to those they serve in light of the vulnerability invited by the professional in the development of the professional fiduciary relationship. Trustworthy professionals also possess at least two "structural" virtues that promote their reliable self-governance in the face of obstacles—integrity and resilience. While integrity and resilience do not aim directly at fulfilling the obligations of trustworthiness, they buttress the other professional virtues.

Loyalty

At one time, the virtue of loyalty was considered *the* distinctive element of professional ethics. When loyal, professionals are disposed to place the client or patient's interests *above their own*. Loyalty is an important virtue for the trustworthy professional because, as argued earlier, there are a variety of conflicts between the interests of the professional and those of his or her clients. Moreover, compliance systems that disincentivize misconduct are only partially effective at promoting reliable care for those who depend on professionals. To be worthy of client and public trust, professionals must have a disposition to set aside the motivational forces of those interests that would tempt them to exploit the vulnerability of those who rely on them. The disposition to do so in one's professional practice is loyalty.

There is, of course, a delicate balance, as professional practice is both an economic activity and a service to others. The relevant virtue falls between utter selflessness and rank egoism. The professional certainly has valid private interests (e.g., financial gain, status), but those who are loyal to the client do not allow their private interests to lead them to fail to responsibly care for the interests that have been entrusted to them. For the loyal professional, private interests are secondary ones that give way to the primacy of the interests entrusted to them by those they serve.

Beneficence

Etymologically, the root of the English word beneficence comes from the Latin term *bene*, which means "good" or "well." In Old English, *bene* meant a prayer, supplication, or favor (as in a benediction). Today the term captures both of these senses. Beneficence is the promotion of the good or welfare of others. In philosophical ethics, it is widely accepted that under certain conditions there is an obligation to beneficence. For instance, when one's actions can prevent significant harm to another person and pose little risk to one's self, ethicists from a wide variety of schools of thought believe that there is an obligation to help. The controversies surrounding the principle of beneficence tend to focus on the range of cases in which beneficence is obligatory as opposed to supererogatory (i.e., morally good, but not required).

Beneficence is inherent in the nature of professional practice as an offer of expert assistance. Professional practice is, in essence, a kind of service to another aimed at promoting his or her well-being in light of an important interest. In medicine, this would be the patient's health; in law, the client's freedom or financial well-being; in engineering, safe and efficient design; in public administration, the efficiency and fairness of state services. As professional practice is an offer of expert assistance, it is an invitation to entrust professionals with discretionary power over important interests of the client.

When clients or the public extend that trust to professionals, a fiduciary relationship is formed; this requires that the professional honors that trust by providing the beneficial service they offered to the client.

As a virtue, beneficence is the character trait by which a professional is motivationally disposed to promote the good of those who depend on them. Along with loyalty, beneficence is perhaps the cardinal virtue of the trustworthy professional because one of the key warrants for inferring trustworthiness is evidence that the trust-candidate is disposed to show good will toward the interests entrusted to him or her. Professionals are judged to be trustworthy in large measure to the degree that clients and the public infer that they are beneficent relative to those whom they serve in their professional practice.

Respect for Client Autonomy

It might be thought that the virtues of professional beneficence and loyalty alone are sufficient for professional trustworthiness, and at one time this was widely assumed to be the case. However, ethicists working in a variety of professions have pointed out that promoting the good of the client cannot be reliably accomplished without respecting the role of the client's decision-making authority. Before the 1970s, it was widely assumed, particularly in fields such as medicine, that professional decision making was exclusively technical. Physicians, it was argued, used medical science to determine the best therapy; lawyers appealed to systems of positive law to determine the best legal recourse for clients; engineers appealed to applied science to determine the best design; and public administrators appealed to law and economics to determine the most efficient administrative practices. In each case, professionals were presumed to be, as Locke once put it about public administrators, "phantoms"[21] that bring expertise, but not personality to their practice.

This idea unraveled in the second half of the twentieth century as it became clear that professional practice was not value free. Take, for example, medicine. Again, before the 1970s, medical decision making was assumed to be purely technical and scientific. Within this model of medical practice, the patient's input and decision making capacity was less than irrelevant. Patients typically lack medical expertise, so their consent to a therapy was not required as a matter of scientific insight or of ethical responsibility. The trust patients placed in their physician was a paternalistic one in which they expected the physician to discover and apply the objectively correct course of treatment.

Critics of the paternalistic paradigm point out that medical decision making is not simply scientific and technical, but involves a healthy dose of values.[22] This is most dramatically seen in "end of life" cases. Is a therapy that will extend life for a few months, but will also likely create significant suffering during that time worth pursuing? This question is simply not a scientific one, but one of *value*. Different persons can reasonably reach different answers on what counts as quality of life and the costs that are reasonable to bear in order to prolong it. The same is true in less dramatic cases in which the side effects of medication must be considered in light of the overall benefit. What counts as "benefit" is rarely an exclusively technical decision. Because risk is inherent in any gain, trade-offs of cost and potential side effects must be weighed in any proposed therapy, and the cost/benefit analysis here is driven at least in part by a value-laden conception of "quality" of life.

Once it was recognized that medical decisions are value-laden, it became clear that the paternalistic model of medical practice was no longer tolerable from a moral (and legal) standpoint. In the 1960s, courts in the United States began ruling that competent individuals have a right to self-determination over what happens to their own bodies, and began finding physicians negligent when they acted without patient consent. In medical ethics, the principle of *autonomy* made a dramatic (and for some, unwelcome) entrance into the discourse and eventually into codes of ethics, law, and medical education. The result has been an impressive sea change regarding the role of the patient in medical decision making. Today many medical ethicists think of medical decision making as a *shared decision-making process* within a deliberative context that includes an entire health care team, as well as the patient, family, and patient advocates. While the process is a shared, deliberative one, decisions are ultimately those of the patient. While it would be wrong to say that "doctor knows best" has been completely replaced with "the patient knows best," the patient has moved to the center of decision making in medicine.

The transformation of the patient-physician relationship has been dramatic, but the lesson is by no means for physicians alone. Professional decisions generally are value-laden ones and, as such, the professional has no right to determine for the client what counts as "beneficial." Therefore, exercising the professional virtue of beneficence cannot be ethically accomplished in a paternalistic fashion. Now that the value-laden nature of professional decisions is widely recognized, paternalistic trust is no longer warranted. Instead, trustworthy professionals recognize the obligation to make the client a central player in the decision-making process, and affectively *respect*, not just grudgingly acknowledge, their self-determination. Of course in some cases, the client may choose to relinquish much of their decision-making authority, but the virtuous professional takes his or her cue from the client on this matter and humbly accepts increased decision-making authority, rather than demanding it.

Honesty

Honesty is routinely cited, both in the professions and in everyday life, as a key disposition of trustworthy individuals. As a virtue, honesty is the disposition to communicate in a nondeceptive and forthright manner with the aim of providing others a genuine understanding of the issue at hand. Honesty entails much more than the avoidance of *lying*. A lie is a communicative act aimed at convincing a listener that a statement, which the speaker believes to be false, is actually true.

Honesty entails more than avoidance of lying because lies are but one form of *deception*. Deception is a communicative act aimed at convincing an audience that a particular state of affairs, which the speaker believes to be false, is actually true (or vice versa). Deception can be achieved with lies, but it can also be achieved with true but misleading statements. For instance, when Bill Clinton was asked if he had an affair with Monica Lewinsky, he responded, "there is no inappropriate relationship." This statement was true, and was therefore not a lie, but it was still dishonest, because it was intended to convince his audience that he had never had an affair with Lewinsky, which was false. Honest communication requires not only the avoidance of lies, but also sufficient *disclosure* of true communication oriented to providing a genuine understanding of the situation at hand.

That honesty is routinely identified as key virtue in those who are trustworthy is not surprising. Deception typically increases the vulnerability of trustors and makes them prone to manipulation. Individuals who are disposed to place others in such precarious conditions seem like unlikely candidates to appropriately care for the interests entrusted to them. Like autonomy, however, honesty has not always been considered an important virtue in the professions. In the paternalistic paradigm of professional practice, the client's input was considered unimportant. As a result, being honest and forthright with the client or the public was not emphasized either as an obligation or virtue.

Again, the most dramatic example of this occurs in medicine. Physicians, for example, would routinely deceive patients, through lies or nondisclosure, about potential side-effects of treatments for fear that if patients were aware of the facts, they would irrationally avoid beneficial, but perhaps painful, treatment. Physicians and medical ethicists generally viewed such deception as justifiable provided it promoted the well-being of the patient. In the paternalistic paradigm of medical practice, beneficence was the cardinal obligation and associated virtue, and if the patient's health was promoted by deception, then such deception was both prudent and ethical. A 1961 survey found that the vast majority (90 percent) of physicians would not inform a patient of a terminal cancer diagnosis because they believed such knowledge would be so emotionally devastating to the patient that the physician's duty to beneficence prohibited an honest disclosure. [23]

With the collapse of the paternalistic paradigm of professional practice, it is now widely recognized in ethics and law that professionals have an obligation to be honest with those who depend on them. Because professional decisions are value-laden ones, appropriately caring for the interests entrusted to the professional requires the decision-making input from clients and the public. Genuine *deliberation* between the professional and those who depend on them requires a disposition on the part of the professional to be honest in their professional practice.

Discretion

In providing expert assistance, professionals routinely acquire sensitive information, the disclosure of which could injure their patients, clients, students, employers, or even the general public. When a professional is trustworthy, he or she has a disposition to treat such information in a discreet fashion. Discretion encompasses the ideas of confidentiality, as well the responsible use of nonconfidential information. [24] In caring for the entrusted interest of sensitive information, the discreet professional recognizes that some information about the client should not be disclosed except in the most exceptional circumstances. This is the idea of *confidentiality* and is rooted in the client's basic right to privacy.

A basic feature of the autonomy of individuals is their right to determine for themselves what information is shared in their various kinds of relationships. [25] This self-determination is undermined in an important way when sensitive information is shared without the client's knowledge or without his or her consent. The most sensitive of this information is protected by the idea of *confidentiality* and is widely recognized in both ethics and law as deserving special protection. The discreet professional recognizes that those they serve must often divulge sensitive information and take on a special vulnerability in relation to the professional. For the discreet professional, this vulnerability serves as a compelling and effective reason to accord such information the highest level of protection.

However, the virtue of discretion also includes a disposition to the responsible care for one's nonconfidential, yet sensitive, information. For example, suppose Jason tells his friend Finn that he has recently filed for divorce. Such information is not, strictly speaking, confidential, as it is a matter of public record. Nonetheless, in trusting Finn, Jason might ascribe to him an obligation to respect the sensitivity of the information and share it responsibly—if at all. Finn might reasonably share this information with his spouse, but if he were to openly discuss it a party, Jason's reactive attitude would, rightly, be one of betrayal.

In responsibly caring for information shared by those whom they serve, trustworthy professionals recognize the sensitivity of even nonconfidential information as a compelling and effective reason to accord this information a special status and treat it in a discreet and sensible manner. Information that could be injurious or even embarrassing to those who depend on professionals should not be casually shared, even if it is a matter of public record.

Diligence and Competence

Recall that one of the conditions of being trustworthy is the competence to perform the actions necessary to care for entrusted interests. When trustworthy relative to a particular action or action domain, agents are competent to responsibly care for the interests entrusted to them. For professionals this means developing the skill set and work habits by which they can be trusted in their professional practice. The virtue of diligence implies effort and care, both in developing the necessary competence to care for the client or public's interest, and in applying the appropriate amount of careful effort to concretize that competence in practice. Diligent professionals take the client's dependence on them as a compelling and effective reason to develop and apply their skills and knowledge so that they can be rationally relied upon to competently care for those who trust them. For this reason, diligent professionals only take on the *kind* of work they are competent to provide, and a *volume* of work that allows them to adequately care for the interests entrusted to them. The importance of developing one's competence cannot be overstated. In engineering ethics, it is often remarked that when engineers fail a client or the public, it is typically because of incompetence, rather than dishonesty or a lack of beneficence.[26]

Integrity

Integrity is one of the most commonly cited virtues in professional ethics, though there is great controversy as to its nature and its status as a virtue. Bernard Williams famously argued that integrity is not a virtue at all because it does not produce motivations to achieve a good, nor does it enable one to develop the right kinds of motivations for action.[27] However, critics point that for Williams "integrity" consists merely of "the extent to which our actions are most deeply ours."[28] A more attractive account of integrity focuses on the agent's capacity to (1) make commitments based on quality deliberative processes, (2) order and organize those commitments into a consistent and coherent moral map, and (3) internalize that moral map into one's identity. When possessing integrity an agent honors rationally endorsed commitments that have been integrated into the agent's life narrative. As a result he or she will be steadfast in honoring those commitments in the face of obstacles. Those with integrity are able to avoid weakness of will and wantonness. Integrity is therefore rightly thought of as a virtue, and as praiseworthy, because it is at the heart of an agent's ability to lead an integrated and coherent life oriented toward flourishing. This makes integrity something of a "structural" virtue in that it describes one's capacity to consistently pursue those values one has thoughtfully developed and integrated into one's life. Structural virtues concern the excellence of self-governance, particularly in the face of obstacles.[29]

Thomas Aquinas argued that there are two central obstacles to the steadfast pursuit of valuable ends—temptation and fear. This is certainly true in the professions, where major causes of misconduct are temptations to place profit, power, or prestige above the interests of the client; and the fear of reprisals that may come from demanding ethical professional practice. The former is common in cases in which professionals abandon loyalty and beneficence because of "conflicts of interest" (which is the subject of chapter 6). The latter occurs in cases in which professionals participate in wrongdoing because they fear the consequences of "rocking the boat."

The capacity to overcome, and perhaps even proactively avoid, these obstacles and remain firm in one's responsible care of the client, patient, or public is the professional virtue of integrity. Those who value their professional commitments and take seriously their obligations to those they serve will want to develop in themselves a principled disposition to remain true to their commitments—to the angels of their better nature—even in the face of temptations and other obstacles to faithful professional practice. Here, the development of temperance and fortitude are important character traits if the professional is to possess integrity. Temperate professionals are principally disposed to control their will such that they are not easily swayed from their ethical commitments to clients, patients, and/or the public by incentivized vice. Such professionals are able to control their appetites for profit, power, and prestige and have the strength of self-control to remain constant in their care of entrusted interests—even when it there is much to gain by abandoning those they serve. Professionals with integrity recognize that it in their true interest to abandon their valued commitments, since doing so does violence to their own identity. Importantly, temperate professionals recognize the dangers created by temptations and seek to avoid arrangements, such as conflicts of interest, which incentivize misconduct.

A second important element of integrity is fortitude, the strength of self-governance to courageously face the risks that come with being an ethical professional. For instance, disclosing serious wronging by one's client or organization (i.e., whistleblowing), confronting an incompetent colleague, pointing out a superior's dangerous mistake, or objecting to an unethical business practice all entail significant risks of formal and informal reprisals. Trustworthy professionals have the fortitude, or moral courage, to overcome the fear of these risks and remain steadfast in the virtuous care of clients, patients, or the public.

Resilience

Temptation and fear are two major causes of professional misconduct, but there is increasing awareness of a third—emotional exhaustion. The contemporary professional works in environments rife with overwork, abuse, high stress, and toxic interpersonal relationships. In health care, nurses are overworked and are routinely abused (sometimes physically) by patients and physicians. In education, teachers and professors face higher workloads, larger class sizes, declining support, and hostile administrators. And in law, chronic overwork and high stress in an antagonistic justice system, and a Machiavellian law firm culture, lead to chronic stress. Professionals also routinely work with "toxic" colleagues who bring true meaning to Sartre's adage "hell is other people."

An important threat to professional trustworthiness comes from the very real possibility of *emotional exhaustion* created by the high stress environments in which professionals work. When emotionally exhausted, professionals lose key empathetic capacities and *depersonalize* those they serve. "The client's problems are not your problems" is a popular expression in many professions. While it is certainly true that a measure of detachment is necessary to cope with the stress of professional practice, when that detachment becomes an emotionally exhausted depersonalization of the client or patient, the "I-Thou" relationship at the heart of the professional's sense of moral accountability and professional flourishing is threatened. The trustworthy professional takes the dependence of others as a compelling reason to responsibly care for the interests entrusted to them, but this attitude is much more difficult to adopt by emotionally exhausted professionals who view the client or patient as an "it" instead of a "Thou."

Given the threats of emotional exhaustion and depersonalization, the trustworthy professional must be *resilient.* In the context of professional practice, resilience is the principled disposition to respond to ongoing work stress and adversity in ways that promote one's individual well-being and professional excellence.[30] As a structural virtue, resilience does not, in and of itself, aim for the care of the client, patient or public. Indeed, the virtue of resilience is very much aimed at *caring for oneself,* which is essential for the sustainably care for others. Virtues appropriately link emotion and practical rationality, thus providing rational insight with motivational support. Emotional exhaustion drains the virtues of their lifeblood, leaving professionals motivationally adrift.

The trustworthy professional not only cares for those they serve, but also engages in a healthy dose of self-care. Importantly, the virtue of resilience does not mean simply being able to absorb an ever-increasing amount of work stress. It means working proactively to *reduce* work stress so that it remains manageable. Resilient professionals therefore develop *healthy* coping mechanisms, social support networks, workload adjustments, and other practices by which they can proactively reduce work stress and reactively manage it when it occurs. Healthy coping mechanisms include the use of mindfulness and meditation techniques; taking time to recognize the value and excellence of one's work and the work of those around you; building social networks inside and outside the workplace so that one can prevent feelings of powerlessness and isolation; exercise and other forms of physical self-care; and activities, such as music, cooking, travel, and writing, that generate "psychological oxygen"—a chance to breathe and experience emotional regeneration.

THE TRUSTWORTHY PROFESSIONAL AND THE TRUSTWORTHY PROFESSION

The trustworthy professional conscientiously takes the dependence of clients, patients, and the public as a compelling and motivationally efficacious reason to responsibly care for the interests entrusted to them. The motivation for such responsible care is driven by principled dispositions—virtues—such as: loyalty, beneficence, honesty, respect for autonomy, discretion, diligence, integrity, and resilience. This simple list of virtues, however, belies the enormous complexities involved in being a trustworthy professional:

1. While many of the virtues of the trustworthy professional are generally and superficially agreed upon, there are many controversies about the precise nature of the professional's fiduciary obligations and the associated virtues that dispose them to honor those obligations.

2. There are also controversies about how these obligations and associated virtues should best be applied in practice. For instance, while some applaud the idea of the client and professional engaging in joint decision making, applying this in practice is challenging because many clients lack the sophistication to meaningfully participate in professional decision making. While very few ethicists and professionals argue we should return to the paternalistic paradigm of professional practice, some argue respecting autonomy and honesty is difficult to realize in practice.

3. To make matters even more complicated, the fiduciary obligations of the professional and their associated virtues are often in tension with one another. For instance, sometimes full disclosure of information is harmful to a patient or client, in which case the professional must choose between promoting beneficence or honesty.

4. The developing of the virtues necessary for trustworthiness require socialization into a particular role, supported by educational institutions and practices that create the kinds of affective responses necessary to create stable character traits.

5. Finally, professionals not only have good reasons to be trustworthy, they have good reasons to be *effectively* trustworthy. This means they not only possess the kinds of dispositions by which they consistently and appropriately respond to the reliance others make on them; they also must effectively *signal* to clients and to the public their possession of trust warranting properties. However, given the relatively anonymous settings in which professionals practice, developing appropriate trust is challenging. On the one hand, the thin conditions of professional practice make trust-building difficult. On the other hand, individuals often make intuitive judgments about trust that are rather superficial and therefore come to trust the wrong sorts of people. Consider the Platonic lament that the wise are often ignored because they speak in a measured and thoughtful manner. Professionals must carefully develop means of generating trust while remaining thoughtful experts. This cannot be done by the professional alone but requires antecedent cues created by the development of the trusted professional social role.

These considerations all point to the idea that the analysis of the trustworthiness of the professional cannot remain in the immediacy of the client-professional relationship. In identifying, interpreting, internalizing, institutionalizing, and communicating the virtues of the trustworthy professional, professionals and clients rely on the broader ethical discourses and institutions supported by the professional community. For this reason, from the perspective of trust and trustworthiness, a distinctive and necessary feature of a profession is that it functions as an *ethical community*. In the next chapter, an account of the profession as an ethical community is developed to show how the discourses and institutions of that community interpret, develop, and signal the trustworthiness of those who occupy professional roles.

CONCLUSION

Professionals have instrumental, ethical, and moral reasons to invite and develop trust on the part of those they serve. From a moral and practical standpoint, the best way to develop such trust is for professionals to be trustworthy. Like trust, trustworthiness can be understood in terms of instrumental and dispositional perspectives. Instrumental accounts of trustworthiness, such as Hardin's model of "interest encapsulation," offer an important resource by which individuals can form trusting relationships under relatively anonymous conditions. However, trust based on interest encapsulation alone is too unstable to generate the kind of reliance necessary for effective professional assistance. Dispositional trustworthiness provides a more secure foundation for client and public trust in professionals. One is trustworthy in this stronger sense when one is disposed to take the vulnerability of the trustor as a compelling and effective reason to responsibly care for their clients, patients, and/or the general public.

In the context of professional practice, trustworthy professionals also possess a variety of character virtues that motivate them to respond favorably and responsibly to the trustor's vulnerability. Virtues such as beneficence, loyalty, honesty, respect for autonomy, discretion, diligence, integrity, and resilience are necessary if professionals are to responsibly care for the interests entrusted to them. However, the professional can neither effectively develop nor signal his or her trustworthiness alone. To create the kind of robust trust necessary for professional practice, a profession must transcend being an economic occupation and become an ethical community.

NOTES

1. Karen Jones, "Trustworthiness," *Ethics* 123, no. 1 (2012): 73. Jones refers to this as "rich trustworthiness."

2. Russell Hardin, *Trust and Trustworthiness* (New York: Russell Sage Foundation, 2002), 2–3.

3. Fyodor Dostoevsky, *The Brothers Karamazov*, trans. David Magarshack (London: Penguin, 1982), 129.

4. Hardin, "Trust and Trustworthiness," 3. See also, Hardin, "Trustworthiness" *Ethics* 107, no. 1 (1996): 26–42.

5. Timothy Simpson, "Trustworthiness and Moral Character," *Ethical Theory and Moral Practice* 16 (2013): 548.

6. Jones, "Trustworthiness," 70.

7. Simpson, 548.

8. Jones, 71.

9. Ibid.

10. Ibid.

11. Williams, "Internal and External Reasons," in *Rational Action*, ed. Ross Harrison (Cambridge, MA: Cambridge University Press, 1979), 101–13.

12. Rosalind Hursthouse, "Virtue Theory," *Stanford Encyclopedia of Philosophy,* accessed March 25, 2016. http://plato.stanford.edu/entries/ethics-virtue/

13. MacIntyre, *After Virtue,* 178.

14. John Dorris, *Lack of Character: Personality and Moral Behavior* (New York: Cambridge University Press, 2002).

15. Gilbert Harman, "The Non-existence of Character Traits," *Proceedings of the Aristotelian Society* 100, 223–26.

16. John Darley and C. Daniel Batson, "From Jerusalem to Jericho: A Study of Situational and Dispositional Variables in Helping Behavior," *Journal of Personality and Social Psychology* 27, no. 1 (1973): 100–108.

17. Jason D'Cruz, "Trust, Trustworthiness, and the Moral Consequence of Consistency," *Journal of the American Philosophical Association* 1, no. 3 (2015). 478–79.

18. C. Daniel Batson, Pamela Cochran, Marshall Beiderman, James Blosser, Maurice Ryan and Bruce Vogt, "Failure to Help When in a Hurry: Callousness or Conflict?" *Personality and Social Psychology Bulletin* 4, no. 1 (1978): 97–101.

19. For an excellent presentation of this line of reasoning against situationism, see Gopol Sreenivasan, "Errors about Errors: Virtue Theory and Trait Attribution," *Mind* 111, no. 441 (2002): 47–68.

20. Bayles, *Professional Ethics,* 2nd ed., 79.

21. John Locke, *Two Treatises of Civil Government* (New York: Cambridge University Press, 1988): 368.

22. For instance see, Robert Veatch, "Is Trust in Professionals a Coherent Concept," in *Ethics, Trust, and the Professions,* ed. Edmund Pellegrino, Robert Veatch and John Lagan (Washington, DC: Georgetown University Press: 1991).

23. L.J. Fallowfield, V.A. Jenkins, and H.A. Beveridge, "Truth May Hurt, but Deceit Hurts More: Communication in Palliative Care," *Palliative Medicine* 16 (2002): 297–303.

24. Bayles, 96.

25. James Rachels, "Why Privacy Is Important," *Philosophy and Public Affairs* 4, no. 4 (1975): 323–33.

26. Mike Martin and Roland Schinzinger, *Ethics in Engineering,* 4th ed., (Boston: McGraw Hill, 2005).

27. Bernard Williams, "Utilitarianism and Self-Indulgence," in *Moral Luck: Philosophical Papers: 1973–1980.* (Cambridge, MA: Cambridge University Press, 1981): 49.

28. Damian Cox, Marguerite La Caze, and Michael Levine, "Should We Strive for Integrity?" *The Journal of Value Inquiry* 33 (1999): 525.

29. Robert Adams, *A Theory of Virtue* (Oxford, UK: Oxford University Press, 2006), 34.

30. Clare McCann, et al., "Resilience in the Health Professions: A Review of Recent Literature." *International Journal of Wellbeing* 3, no. 1 (2013): 61.

Chapter Four

The Profession as an Ethical Community

In a number of key respects the professional cannot become effectively trustworthy alone. As Aristotle rightly argued, character development is an intersubjective process by which individuals, in the context of community, develop through education and habituation, reliable practical insight, as well as proper affective responses to that insight. Moreover, the obligations and virtues of the trustworthy professional are open to a variety of interpretations and debates requiring a broader ethical discourse linked to decision-making institutions. Finally, effective professional trustworthiness requires the signaling of one's reliability in relatively anonymous conditions. When inviting and developing anonymous trust, professionals appeal to the reputation of their social role. Such reputation cannot be developed by the individual professional alone, but requires the concerted actions of professionals and professional institutions working together. For these reasons, professionals can be effectively trustworthy only as members of robust ethical communities that: (1) conduct ongoing justificatory and interpretive discourses which justify and apply the duties and virtues of the trustworthy professional; (2) develop the professional character virtues of its members through education and discipline; and (3) promote and communicate the reputation of the professional social role.

ETHICAL COMMUNITY AND DISCOURSE

A community is a group of individuals united by a set of commitments, values, and practices that are institutionalized in such a way that the community transcends the mere collection of its current individual members. A community is therefore more than an aggregate of individuals with similar ideas or values, but an intersubjective and dynamic accomplishment in which individuals mutually recognize one another as partners in a joint project.

An *ethical* community is one in which the values, commitments, and practices in question relate to a telos which community members endorse as a valuable form of excellence or flourishing. In an ethical community, community members cooperatively engage in projects that promote the community telos. By doing so, community members hold one another accountable for praise or blame based on an understanding of the obligations and virtues implied by that telos.

An important way in which ethical communities are institutionalized is through the development and maintenance of a discourse in which community members exchange claims on a wide variety of issues related to the community telos and its promotion. This kind of discourse has been characterized as "ethical/existential" because it focuses not on the rights and obligations of all persons qua persons, but rather on the interpretation and implementation of a particular telos consciously pursued only by members of the community. Discourses that focus on the exchange and evaluation of validity claims regarding the rights and obligations of persons as such are "moral" as opposed to "ethical/existential." [1]

Ethical/existential discourses differ from moral ones in the scope of the questions considered, but also in the audience addressed. In moral discourses, validity claims are offered, in principle, for the consideration and evaluation of all persons, with an aim at generating a rational consensus based on the forceless force of the better argument. In ethical/existential discourse, claims are addressed primarily at fellow community members with the aim of generating consensus within the community itself. Because validity claims in an ethical/existential discourse are premised on the acceptance of a consciously pursued telos not necessarily shared by those outside the community, ethical/existential discourse aims for community, not universal, consensus.

Perhaps the clearest illustration of an ethical community is found in religion. In a religious community, members are united by a consciously pursued telos and participate in an ongoing ethical discourse about the nature of that telos. They consider how it is best practiced by individual members and institutionalized in the community itself. The claims exchanged by religious community members are premised on the accepted validity of the community telos; as such the arguments exchanged in support of those claims are relative to the community's value framework. As a result, a religious community might have standards of praise and blame that members are expected to endorse—standards particularized relative to the faith-based value framework adopted by community members.

Professions are also ethical communities. Indeed, the idea of a profession comes in part via the idea that those in such communities "profess" to serve a higher goal such as justice, health, or education. As an ethical community, professionals are united by the conscious pursuit of a telos or defining end. They believe this end to be valuable and are willing to adopt it as the primary criterion for determining standards of praise and blame within the community. To this end, they develop and maintain an ongoing discourse in which validity claims are exchanged among members of the profession with an eye toward generating a community consensus on issues of interpreting and implementing the community telos. For instance, physicians are united by their commitment to the fundamental value of promoting and restoring health and relieving suffering, and they engage in discourse aimed as interpreting and promoting that telos.

The simple statement of the medical telos as "promoting and restoring health and alleviating suffering" belies enormous complexity and indeterminacy. Consider the question of what constitutes "health." There are a wide variety of schools of thought as to what constitutes "health," ranging from approaches that focus on the statistical norms of physical functioning, to approaches that incorporate spirituality. A similar point can be made about law. While it may seem obvious that the telos of the legal profession is the promotion of justice, the question "what is justice?" is as old as philosophy itself. Should justice be understood substantively or procedurally? Does it amount to "winning" (as in adversarial legal systems) or "finding the truth" (as in more inquisitorial systems)?

The indeterminacy of the professional telos requires professional communities to face fundamental existential questions: "Who are we? What is our defining end and the core values that we promote?" Ethical communities address such questions in an ongoing interpretive and justificatory discourse that, over time—indeed over generations—develops provisional and revisable interpretations of the core telos of the community and how to achieve it.

There are, however, key differences between the professions and other ethical communities, such as religious communities. Unlike religious communities, professional communities exist to serves clients and the public. They have ethical and *moral* responsibilities to care for the vulnerabilities of others in an adequate fashion and to promote important social goods. As a result, the professional ethical/existential discourse cannot be entirely self-referential, but must be open to the broader moral discourse that considers what agents owe one another as persons. Standards of praise and blame within the professional community cannot be entirely relativized to the consciously pursued telos of that community, but must also satisfy the standards of moral rightness that all persons deserve. Professional norms such as non-malfeasance, honesty, and respect for client autonomy are, therefore, not only ethical community standards, they are basic rights owed to all persons who extend their trust to professionals. Indeed, much of professional ethics is ultimately grounded on basic rights and duties of all persons, not only members of a particular community. Moreover, because the professions serve the public in a pluralistic society, its moral obligations trump its ethical sense of authenticity—as Rawls famously puts it, the right has "priority" over the good.[2] For these reasons, professionals may not use their community telos as a legitimate rationale for violating the moral rights of their clients or the public at large.

Because they must be guided by moral reasoning in many respects it is tempting to think that professional communities simply engage in moral discourse; that is, that they are merely a part of the broader discourse that aims at determining what is owed to others from a universal perspective. However, professional discourse is distinct from moral discourse in a number of important respects. While professionals have a moral obligation to honor the rights of others as persons, professional communities also explore, within the realm of that which is morally permissible there is broad opportunity for ethical/existential interpretation and implementation of the community telos. For instance, in the physician-assisted suicide debate, one might, from the moral perspective, conclude that it is permissible for individuals to terminate their lives under the appropriate circumstances, and to enlist others to assist them. At the same time, one might conclude, as the *American Medical Association* has, that it is inappropriate for *physicians* to assist a patient's suicide because such an act is alien to essence of the physician-role as healer.

Professional discourses are best thought of as *ethico-moral* given the interpenetration of moral and teleological considerations when justifying professional norms of conduct. "Justification" discourses must also be distinguished from "application" discourses within the professions. *Application discourses* consider the appropriate manner in which norms are applied to a practice given the normative and pragmatic demands of the context.[3] In the professions, application discourses take on the pragmatic task of determining how the outcomes of ethico-moral justificatory discourse are to be appropriately applied in the unique context of professional practice. For instance, the justificatory (moral and ethical) discourse in the medical profession broadly supports the idea that patient autonomy entails the right to adequate disclosure of information that promotes intelligent patient decision making. But *applying* the norm "adequate disclosure" raises questions regarding the most *appropriate* manner of such disclosure given the unique context of medical care.

In some medical situations, for example, full and immediate disclosure might disable the autonomous decision-making abilities of the patient, and in some extreme cases can materially harm the patient (e.g., cause cardiac arrest). Fulfilling the obligation to respect and promote patient autonomy requires careful consideration of the appropriate mode of action. For instance, the *American Medical Association* now endorses the idea that in some circumstances "staged disclosure" may be an appropriate mode of providing information to a patient.[4] In staged disclosure, information is provided to the patient in a manner and in intervals that allow the patient to make the best possible decision at each stage. The goal is reasonably adequate disclosure, but done in a manner and by timing that supports, rather than overwhelms, the autonomy of the patient.

Thinking through appropriate disclosure standards is a project taken up by the community of practitioners most familiar with the practical challenges of the professional context. Staged disclosure may be occasionally appropriate in medicine, but it is unlikely that it would ever be appropriate in engineering since information disclosed by engineers rarely has the disabling effect on employers or clients that grievous medical information can have on patients. While justificatory discourse might support the idea of autonomy and adequate disclosure of information, the application discourses of each professional community must address the appropriate means of fulfilling the outcomes of moral discourse in light of the contexts in which each profession is practiced. For this reason, professional role obligations are not only distinct from one's ordinary obligations; they are also, in practice, distinct from one profession to the next.

Justificatory and application discourses work interactively. Justified norms and principles must be interpreted in application discourses in order to gain concrete content. At the same time, the results of application discourse must remain open to critical feedback from justificatory discourse. For instance, the issue of "staged disclosure" while developed within the application discourse of the medical community, must remain subject to scrutiny from the broader public moral discourse. Objections that such forms of disclosure unjustly violate the patient's right to autonomy or constitute a betrayal of trust must become an input to be considered by a responsible medical discourse.

THE PROFESSIONAL COMMUNITY AND THE CULTURE OF TRUST

As an ethical community, a profession engages in a variety of discourses that identify, interpret, and implement the appropriate modes of conduct and character education within the profession in light of the ongoing interpretation of the professional telos. As a result, professional discourse plays a central role in the creation of a *culture of trust* by symbolically orienting professional role-expectations in ways that promote trustworthy dispositions on the part of professional practitioners, and by considering and developing ways to ensure alignment between the existential self-understanding of professionals and the care required for those they serve. One way professional communities promote the development of trustworthy professionals is through the symbolic construction and institutionalization of the "professional-role holder" as one who strives to be worthy of client and public trust.

Self-understanding is situated within a horizon of shared meanings, narratives, roles, and other symbolic constructions. Professional discourses can play a constitutive role in the symbolically mediated self-understanding of the professional qua professional by shaping the meaningful horizon of professional practice in ways that highlight the moral, ethical, and instrumental importance of trust and the virtues necessary for trustworthiness. The goal of such communicative orientation is to integrate the idea of the "professional" and the "trustworthy professional" via the creation of a self-understanding of the professional that is morally and ethically grounded. Maintaining a robust discourse by highlighting morality and ethics in professional journals, conferences, training, and "everyday" office communication helps create a normatively robust self-understanding on the part of individual professionals. Moreover, the normative basis of the professional community itself can be symbolically explained, defined, and promoted in mission statements and codes of ethics of professional organizations and institutions. When successful, a professional community is able to define what it means to be a professional in such a manner that community members consider trustworthiness as every bit as essential to their role as technical competence.

Codes of ethics are a particularly interesting—and controversial—way that professional communities define and promote the central role of trustworthiness in the symbolic construction of professional role identity. With various professions experiencing scandals that have placed their trustworthiness in question, the number of ethics codes has skyrocketed—along with critiques of those codes as mere window dressing that ineffectively promotes ethical professional behavior.[5] One problem with the use of ethical codes is that their value is generally misunderstood, and this misunderstanding reflects a broader, problematic, trend in professional ethics. Professional ethics has drifted toward a "compliance paradigm" in which professional responsibility is understood in terms of compliance with a set of specific rules of conduct, rather than in terms of the development of virtuous dispositions.

THE COMPLIANCE PARADIGM OF PROFESSIONAL ETHICS

Codes of ethics are widely utilized as external constraints upon the professional, aimed at obliging compliance with a set of specific rules prohibiting various forms of inappropriate behavior. Understood this way, they reflect the idea that professional responsibility is best grounded on instrumental trustworthiness—the idea that someone is trustworthy when his or her self-interests encapsulate the interests of those who trust them. When there is insufficient alignment of interests between parties, advocates of instrumental trustworthiness argue that institutional constraints can be used to create external inducements that introduce new incentives (or disincentives, as the case may be) to create interest encapsulation. Using ethics codes as external inducements is part of a broader instrumental strategy that promotes compliance in professional ethics. In the compliance paradigm, the motivation for complying with such rules relies on disciplinary mechanisms that punish noncomplying professionals.

However noble the intention, such an understanding of professional ethics is not effective in creating the kinds of dispositions on the part of professionals that would make them sufficiently trustworthy given the knowledge and power asymmetries at the heart of the fiduciary professional-client/public relationship. Certainly, disciplinary penalties can and do provide powerful motivations for professionals to comply with, or at least not *openly and blatantly* violate, professional rules of conduct. However, the entire compliance paradigm is a hedging strategy that aims for the best of the worst-case outcome. Demanding compliance with rules of conduct is unlikely to create dispositionally trustworthy professionals, although it at least provides motivations for professionals to meet *minimal* standards of care. However, such a hedging strategy comes with a variety of costs:

1. The compliance paradigm promotes the idea that rule following is an adequate basis for ethical action, and in no way addresses the underlying *character* of the professional. Without the development of dispositional trustworthiness and its associated professional virtues—such as loyalty, beneficence, honesty, discretion, diligence, and respect for autonomy—the professional's trustworthiness is unstably grounded on the professional's *fear* of being caught and punished for unethical behavior. However, given the knowledge asymmetries in professional relationships, professionals are often in the position of Gyges from Plato's *Republic*, whose invisible ring allowed him to escape the consequences for his unjust behavior. Because the work of professionals cannot be completely policed, clients and the public often rely on them in the absence of surveillance. The result is that professionals routinely need not fear being caught when engaging in unethical behavior. Moreover, many professionals are notoriously reluctant to discipline peers, effectively removing an important incentive within the compliance paradigm to ensure that professionals are trustworthy.

2. As enforced rule following, the compliance paradigm promotes a legalistic interpretation of the rules that equates ethical action with

adherence to a formal understanding of the rule. Professionals are consequently encouraged to focus on the letter of the rule and not the underlying ethical and moral rationale, or "spirit," behind it. This in turn encourages "loophole" reasoning in which professionals perceive "ethics" as a matter of not violating the strict letter of the rule. If one adopts the view "that which is not forbidden is permitted," then the gray areas in the rules become gaps that unscrupulous professionals exploit for personal gain at the expense of the client or public.

3. A common response to loophole reasoning is to increase the specific-ity of the rules of conduct, with the result of making the code of ethics a "code" in the worst possible sense. The code becomes lengthy, com-plex and legalistic—indeed, many ethics codes require legal training to adequately understand and apply. In some cases, this makes follow-ing the code difficult even for conscientious professionals who must seek out the expert advice of their ethics officer or ethics board simply to understand what the code means.

4. Because the motivation for compliance is external constraint, many professionals perceive "ethics" as an alien feature imposed on them. Perversely, instead of serving as a source of self-esteem and mutual recognition, ethics becomes a source of resentment and alienation. Many professionals come to think of professional ethics as an artificial system of disciplinary rules that are completely distinct from morality.

5. Because the motivation for ethical behavior is fear of disciplinary reprisal, professional practice often becomes "defensive," in that ethi-cally serving the client, employer, or public becomes a matter of meeting the *minimum* care required by the rules. This "checkbox" mentality often fails to adequately honor the client's trust because it fails to promote the responsible care of client or public. Instead it promotes conduct that will avoid discipline, which is not necessarily coextensive with conduct that protects the client or public.

It is little wonder then that ethics code seem to have little, if any, appreciable effect on the quality of professional behavior. When understood as an exter-nal constraint on behavior, ethics codes fail in two ways: they do not address the character of professionals and, at the same time, they promote a defensive attitude in which "ethics" is an alien, and alienating element to their profes-sional practice.

THE AUTHENTICITY PARADIGM OF PROFESSIONAL ETHICS

Developing trustworthy professionals requires moving beyond the compliance paradigm to the creation of a genuine *culture of trust*[6] in the professional community and the organizational contexts of professional practice. What is needed is a professional ethics that emphasizes the development of dispositional trustworthiness through an internalized professional identity anchored in the professional virtues. In such an approach—the *authenticity paradigm* of professional ethics—the warrant for moral and ethical action is not external to the professional, but resides in his or her sense of authenticity and self-esteem. Professional ethical standards become a basis for personal self-esteem as well as mutual recognition of members within the profession. Understood in this paradigm, the function and design of professional ethics codes are quite different from in the compliance paradigm.

The practical discourses of the professional community are essential to identifying and interpreting the virtues necessary for professionals to be worthy of client and public trust. Understood as an ethical/existential expression, the discursive construction of the professional role, when successful, gives professionals powerful reasons to develop trustworthy dispositions because the commitment to being trustworthy is a key element of their authentic professional identity. When the professional's self-identify is successfully mediated through a discourse oriented toward the development of trustworthiness, violations of professional norms would be tantamount to a violation of *oneself*. Unlike the compliance paradigm, which depends on external constraints to motivate behavior, the authenticity paradigm makes the reasons for being trustworthy *internal* ones in that they emanate from the professional's own sense of self-worth.

In the authenticity paradigm, codes of ethics are ethical/existential statements of communal self-understanding, which are concrete products of the ongoing ethical discourse supported by the profession in an effort to identify and interpret its telos along with the obligations that flow from the invitation to trust that is extended to the public in light of that telos. In other words, a code of ethics offers an opportunity for a community to take stock of itself and commit to an ethico-moral view of what it means to be a member of that professional community.

When understood as a matter of ethical/existential identification, codes of ethics are more appropriately designed as aspirational principles rather than specific rules of conduct. These principled statements should identify the general obligations of the professional as well as the associated virtues that make for excellent professional conduct. Moreover, the code should not be presented uncoupled from the reasoning that gives meaning and legitimacy to those principles. Professional rules of conduct are rules of reason that flow from professional responsibilities and should be presented as such. Identifying oneself with a set of principles requires seeing their inner reason at work in them, and this is best accomplished by presenting aspirational principles with their underlying justification.

Finally, the code must be presented in the context and with the support of robust ethical discourse within the profession. Ethics codes are important statements of professional self-understanding, but they are not the only means by which the profession reflects ethically upon itself. In its ongoing ethico-moral discourse, the professional community gives life to the code by continuing the rational exploration and promotion of the ethical and moral nature of the professional role. Ethics codes are but one part of this effort, but must be given life by the community's discursive and institutional commitment to create a *culture* that reflects the code. Without this holistic approach, an ethics code quickly becomes mere "window dressing" that is unrelated to the reality of professional practice.

While the ongoing practical discourse of the professional community is essential in developing the disposition necessary for trustworthiness on the part of professionals, it cannot do so alone. An effective discourse requires a practical context that meets it halfway. A true culture of trust requires robust practical discourses that are successfully linked to professional institutions, such that the lived experience of the professional reflects and reinforces the discursively constructed professional identity.

FROM DISCURSIVE LEGITIMACY TO PRACTICAL CREDIBILITY

One reason why ethics codes can be ineffective is that the values they express, and kinds of reasons that justify those values are alien to the everyday practice of the professional. This is especially true in competitive professions such as law and financial services where strategic reasoning is given a privileged place in both the training and practice of the professional. The result is that the ethical and moral reasoning essential to the development of trustworthy dispositions lacks *practical credibility*. Practical credibility is the intuitive legitimacy that a practice has in light of its consistency with accepted and familiar features of the one's action domain. Routinized practices, conventions, habits, strategies, and institutional arrangements of professional life have a powerful ordinariness to them, and this ordinariness lends them credibility because the practices and the perspectives they engender become "common sense."

If the development of trustworthy dispositions on the part of professionals is to be successful, the discursive construction of the virtuous profession must be made indigenous to the practical field so that it gains practical credibility with professionals. Without practical credibility, the link between the discursive construction of the "trustworthy professional" and the "common sense" of actual professionals will be too weak to give professionals internal reasons to develop the dispositions needed to become trustworthy. The ethical discourse maintained by the professional community needs to be effectively coupled with decision-making institutions within the profession in order to create a moral ecology which is supportive of, rather than toxic to, the dispositions necessary for professionals to be trustworthy.

Because practical credibility is shaped by formative experiences, professional education and training is an important site, perhaps the most important site, for establishing practices and perspectives that promote the practical credibility of the discursively constructed "trustworthy professional." Educational institutions should consider how faculty selection, curricular design, and clinical experiences can not only foster technical competence, but create an action context for young professionals that lends practical credibility to the development and exercise of trustworthy dispositions. For instance, faculty members teaching in professional programs are important role models and moral exemplars who can normalize and lend practical credibility to ethical practices through their own professional practice. For this reason, professional educational institutions have good reason to assess prospective faculty members not only in terms of the technical competence, but also in light of the ethical quality of their professional practice.

Discourse and Practical Credibility in Nursing

A good example of integrating the discursive construction of the trustworthy professional and the practical credibility of *being* such a professional comes from the nursing profession. Nursing is widely regarded as a trustworthy profession, and much can be learned about the way the nursing community promotes this trustworthiness. The ethico-moral discourse conducted by the nursing community is an excellent illustration of the importance and power of a professional community's capacity to create a symbolically mediated self-understanding for its members.

Traditionally, nurses have been viewed as auxiliaries of physicians in a highly vertical, structured authority relationship. The role of the nurse was to carry out the commands of the physicians and to provide emotional support and care for patients. As Lisa Newton points out, the very concept of "nursing" has its roots in the mother's nursing of her infant child.[7] Whereas the physician-father provides intellectual direction to the care of the patient, the nurse-mother provides the direct physical and emotional care of the patient. For much of its history, nursing was not considered a profession because nurses were thought to lack the intellectual skills and autonomy that were the hallmarks of the paradigmatic professions such as law, medicine, and ministry.

This division of labor, with the physician as the head and the nurse as the heart of patient care, has undergone sustained criticism over the last thirty years. Because nurses and not doctors spend significant amounts of time with patients, they are often in a better position to determine the efficacy of treatment and potential courses of action to improve patient care. Moreover, nurses play a significant role in detecting medical errors and ineffective therapies.[8] The epistemic value of the nurse's perspective, however, was lost in the traditional role-construction of the nurse as a subservient assistant to the physician.

Throughout the late nineteenth and early twentieth century nursing developed into a professional community. The first nursing schools in the United States were established in the 1870s and early professional associations in the 1890s. The *American Journal of Nursing* was first published in 1900. In 1938 New York State required registered nurses to be licensed, and in 1950 the American Nursing Association (ANA) adopted the Code for Professional Nurses. Despite these professional developments, the traditional understanding of the nurse persisted well into the twentieth (indeed even the twenty-first) century.

Throughout the 1970s, significant debates occurred within the nursing community critical of the traditional understanding of nursing and seeking to create a new, more professional and autonomous nursing role that could better serve patients and reflect the increasing sophistication and technical expertise of the modern nurse. The result was an important shift in the community's self-understanding from "nurse-as-caregiver" to "nurse-as-patient-advocate."[9] Providing care to patients is a key component of being a patient advocate, but patient advocacy emphasizes that the nurse's primary telos is *not* serving the physician, but ensuring quality care for the patient. Understood as an advocate, the nurse has an obligation to *assert* a certain measure of autonomy to ensure that his or her patient is well cared for. This advocacy model has become a core element in the new nursing code of ethics (adopted in 2001) and is ubiquitous in nursing education and professional literature today. The result is that the nursing community has successfully created a new existential self-understanding for community members, one that emphasizes patient-advocacy and the need for professional autonomy and assertiveness.

The ANA's new nursing code of ethics is a reflection of this new self-understanding and offers important lessons on how to utilize an ethics code holistically within the authenticity paradigm of professional ethics. The nursing code of ethics is relatively easy to understand, consisting of nine key principles (as opposed to rules) that outline what is expected of the ethically competent nurse:

1. The nurse, in all professional relationships, practices with compassion and respect for the inherent dignity, worth, and uniqueness of every individual, unrestricted by considerations of social or economic status, personal attributes, or the nature of health problems.

2. The nurse's primary commitment is to the patient, whether an individual, family, group, or community.

3. The nurse promotes, advocates for, and strives to protect the health, safety, and rights of the patient.

4. The nurse is responsible and accountable for individual nursing practice and determines the appropriate delegation of tasks consistent with the nurse's obligation to provide optimum patient care.

5. The nurse owes the same duties to self as to others, including the responsibility to preserve integrity and safety, to maintain competence, and to continue personal and professional growth.

6. The nurse participates in establishing, maintaining, and improving health-care environments and conditions of employment conducive to the provision of quality health care and consistent with the values of the profession through individual and collective action.

7. The nurse participates in the advancement of the profession through contributions to practice, education, administration, and knowledge development.

8. The nurse collaborates with other health professionals and the public in promoting community, national, and international efforts to meet health needs.

9. The profession of nursing, as represented by associations and their members, is responsible for articulating nursing values, for maintaining the integrity of the profession and its practice, and for shaping social policy.[10]

The code is aspirational and understandable. Moreover, it is offered in conjunction with commentary that aims to explain the justification and rationale for the various principles. This helps avoid the pitfalls of legalistic rule following and the "loophole" and "box check" mentalities. The nursing professional also avoids the mistake of using its ethics code directly as an external constraint to enforce adherence to minimal standards. The aspirational principles of the code serve as the basis for a wide variety of policies and practices that concretize the principles in the professional social field. The code, for example, articulates the orientation of ethics education within nursing programs, which has a positive influence on the moral confidence, competence, and action of nursing students.[11] Nursing programs also use their ethics code and ethics education in conjunction with "Good Moral Character" (GMC) requirements in which the aspirational principles articulated in the code are understood in terms of the ethical disposition necessary for the competent nurse.

GMC in nursing is defined in terms of virtues such as honesty, integrity, trustworthiness, reliability, accountability, and the ability to distinguish right from wrong.[12] In many nursing programs, students are required to sign a contract indicating their understanding that, and commitment to, the idea that GMC is a basic expectation of competent nursing and is therefore a necessary component of nursing training. Admission into nursing programs, assessment of the student's educational performance, and graduation from nursing programs contain important elements in which GMC is assessed and factored into grades and the student's overall standing in the program. For instance, plagiarism and other forms of academic dishonesty are taken as indications of insufficient dispositional honesty for one to serve as a competent nurse and can lead to failing grades, suspension, and even removal from the program.

Because, as in many professions, certified nursing programs are gatekeepers to entry into the field, the development and demonstration of GMC is a necessary requirement for one to become a professional nurse. This is especially true because in most states, GMC requirements within nursing programs work hand-in-hand with state licensing agencies that also appeal to GMC criteria in licensing and disciplining nurses. Nursing programs proactively use GMC expectations to develop the range of dispositions necessary for nurses to be trustworthy, while licensing agencies use GMC requirements as an external inducement to further incentivize the development of those dispositions.

By onboarding nursing candidates through GMC requirements, the profession takes the discursively constructed vision of the ethically and morally competent nurse as articulated in its aspirational code of ethics, and concretizes it in the everyday practice of the nursing student. By linking the linguistically mediated nursing-role with the practical field of the nursing student, the role is materialized and can be endorsed both from the perspectives of discursive rationality and practical credibility.

Assessments of GMC focus on the *conduct* of the student and thus take a "thin" view of character as a pattern of conduct. However, the professional virtues are rooted in character in a "thick" sense—as stable, principled dispositions anchored in personality traits of the individual.[13] Consequently, GMC requirements and assessment must work hand in hand with curriculum and pedagogy that promotes the professional virtues of the student's "thick" character. Ethics education, in both stand-alone courses *and* integrated in clinical experiences, guided by faculty role-models who are themselves exemplars of GMC is a necessary part of successful nursing education. In the "stair step" approach to nursing ethics education, students begin with a formal, rules-based, understanding of nursing ethics. Curriculum and pedagogy is then designed to move the nursing student from this formal understanding of what nurses ought to "do," to a richer understanding of who a nurse ought to "be." Students are encouraged, through ethics-oriented clinical training and role modeling, to internalize the values of ethical nursing and form a strong professional nursing identity—to *become* good nurses.[14] This onboarding process is buttressed by the cultivation of the value of lifelong learning by which nurses internalize the idea that their skills—both technical and ethical—require ongoing education throughout their professional careers, lest they atrophy and lead to incompetence.

Stair step and GMC onboarding in nursing shows how professional communities can integrate discursive legitimacy with practical credibility. A wide variety of professions are in a position to utilize stair step training and GMC assessment to integrate the discursively legate conception of ethical professional practice with the practical credibility necessary for this conception to become dispositional. Teacher, law, counseling, and engineering education, for example, provide opportunities to integrate ethics training into formal coursework and operationalize that training through internships guided by mentors who are exemplars of both technical expertise and trustworthy character. By enriching the educational ethos to include emphasis and internalization of the relevant lifelong character virtues, professional training programs can transcend mere compliance with ethical rules and can develop dispositionally trustworthy professionals.

DISPOSITIONAL *AND* INSTRUMENTAL TRUSTWORTHINESS IN THE PROFESSIONS

While "authenticity paradigm" focuses on the importance of dispositional trustworthiness, it would be a mistake to think that it has no place for instrumental trustworthiness and the use of institutional constraints on behavior. Sadly, even well-designed ethics programs and GMC training and assessment cannot guarantee that all members of the professional community will have the character necessary to be dispositionally trustworthy. Some will not be dispositionally trustworthy at all, while others only partially so. Professional communities must therefore work to buttress character-based education with mechanisms that ensure instrumental trustworthiness. In fact, the implementation of character-based education is often intertwined with efforts to promote instrumental trustworthiness as well.

The nursing community, for instance, promotes instrumental trustworthiness by *requiring* compliance with GMC in its education, licensing and disciplining of nurses. In the educational setting, enforcing GMC serves not only as an external inducement to avoid misconduct, it also demonstrates to nursing students the importance that GMC has to the practice of nursing. Indeed, if nursing programs did not require evidence of GMC, this would create the (not unreasonable) impression that the discursive endorsement of GMC was mere window dressing. By *requiring* demonstration of GMC in educational settings, nursing programs reinforce the idea that an ethical orientation and trustworthy dispositions are essential to the self-understanding of anyone who thinks of himself or herself as a "professional nurse." When successful, nursing programs produce nurses who are trustworthy both dispositionally and instrumentally.

By working with state regulatory agencies, the nursing community is also able to use GMC as an *external* inducement for those nurses who have not developed trustworthy dispositions or whose character is such that an occasional "nudge" helps them remain steadfast in times of temptation. For this reason, conduct indicative of insufficient moral character can be a cause for discipline—even if the conduct takes place outside of the professional context.[15]

Such practices highlight the importance of GMC and give nurses good reasons to view the development and exercise of trustworthy dispositions as practically credible—and prudent from an instrumental perspective. This better positions the community to avoid the pitfalls of the compliance paradigm of professional ethics while capitalizing on the important effect that external inducements can have in creating interest encapsulation. While compliance as the *paradigm* of professional ethics is insufficient, compliance schemes, and the instrumental trustworthiness they promote, serve a valuable function by offering some protection to patients from unethical nurses and offering a reinforcing incentive to good nurses whose character is tested in moments of weakness or temptation.

TRUSTWORTHINESS AND PROFESSIONAL INSTITUTIONS

The case of GMC development in nursing also highlights the central role played by professional institutions, especially professional associations and professional educational institutions. One of the hallmarks of professional communities is that they are anchored in associations by which community members organize professional practice. As key players in this community, the members—and especially the leadership—of professional institutions and associations have good reasons to promote the kind of discourse, policies, and practical context by which trustworthiness is both discursively legitimate and practically credible for the rank and file professional. For instance, professional associations, because they represent the professional community at large, and because of the unique role they play in developing the community's ethico-moral discourse, have a special obligation to promote the requisite ethical culture within the profession that makes its members generally trustworthy. For this reason, professional associations cannot be mere trade associations focused on promoting the profitability of the profession. Professional associations are anchors of the profession as an ethical community and should act as such.

Professional educational institutions likewise play an important role in developing the trustworthiness of members of the profession. They therefore have an obligation to give ethics training—especially character development—the important place it deserves in professional education. Professional educational institutions should also carefully consider the selection of faculty members in light of the examples they might serve as character role models and mentors for students.

Finally, professional workplaces should be organized in a way that promotes the development and maintenance of dispositional and instrumental trustworthiness on the part of professionals. Firms, hospitals, court systems, and schools need to be structured in a way so that the practical culture of the professional gives practical credibility to and nourishes trustworthiness, rather than erodes it. Many professionals work in conditions that are not conducive to the development and exercise of the professional virtues. In nursing, understaffing and "floating" make it more difficult for nurses to promote the well-being of their patients; overcrowded classrooms make it difficult for teachers to remain emotionally engaged with their students; and cut-throat politics in the law firm make it difficult for lawyers to take ethical dispositions seriously. These ethically alienating conditions increase the risk of professionals becoming "emotionally exhausted" and depersonalizing those who rely on them. [16]

The effect of an ethically toxic culture can cause widespread damage in the profession itself. The nursing profession, for example, is experiencing a crisis as nurses leave the profession in droves due to "moral distress"—the condition by which they recognize the kind of care owed to patients, but believe the workplace environment prevents it. [17] Nurses who suffer from repeated moral distress—called "moral residue"—typically burn out and either leave the field or become emotionally exhausted, thus losing the disposition to *care* for patients.

Given the damage caused by ethically toxic workplace environments, professional associations, educational institutions, and professional enterprises have good reasons to create a concerted community approach to the development of the kind of discourse, training, credentialing, and workplace domain that promotes and supports the trustworthy professional. The development of the trustworthy professional is not only a requirement of justice, but it ultimately promotes the existential self-fulfillment of professionals, and the bottom line of professional enterprises.

CONCLUSION

Developing trustworthiness on the part of the professions requires the work of the profession as an ethical community. In such communities, justification and application discourses interpret the professional telos, determine the obligations and virtues required by professional practice, and judge how these are best applied in the practical context of the profession. Good moral character criteria in professional education, licensing, and discipline bring the community's ethical insights into the concrete reality of the professional's life. Such approaches promote trustworthiness by developing the appropriate character virtues on the part of professionals. When successful, professions as ethical communities are able to create a discourse and practical context that lends legitimacy and practical credibility to the idea of *being* a trustworthy professional.

NOTES

1. Jürgen Habermas, "On the Pragmatic, Ethical and Moral Employments of Practical Reason," in *Justification and Application*, trans. and ed. Ciaran Cronin (Cambridge, MA: MIT Press, 1993), 1–19.

2. John Rawls, *Justice as Fairness: A Restatement*, ed. by Erin Kelly. (Cambridge, MA: Belknap Press, 2001), 82.

3. See Habermas, "On the Pragmatic, Ethical and Moral Employments of Practical Reason." See also, Klaus Gunthar, *The Sense of Appropriateness* (New York: SUNY Press, 1993).

4. *American Medical Association*, "Opinion 8.082—Withholding Information from Patients," http://www.ama-assn.org/ama/pub/physician-resources/medical-ethics/code-medical-ethics/opinion8082.page?

5. See, John Dienhart, "Rationality, Ethical Codes, and an Egalitarian Justification of Ethical Expertise: Implications for Professions and Organizations," *Business Ethics Quarterly* 5, no. 3 (1995): 419–50. See also, John Dobson, "Monkey Business: A neo-Darwinist Approach to Ethics Codes," *Financial Analysts Journal* 61, no. 3 (2005): 59–64.

6. Andrew Brian, "Professional Ethics and the Culture of Trust," *Journal of Business Ethics* 17, no. 4 (1998): 392.

7. Lisa Newton, "In Defense of the Traditional Nurse," *Nursing Outlook* 29, no. 6 (1981): 348–54.

8. Helga Kuhse, *Caring: Nurses, Women and Ethics* (New York: Wiley-Blackwell, 1997).

9. Gerald Winslow, "From Loyalty to Advocacy: A New Metaphor for Nursing," *Hastings Center Report* 14, no. 3 (1984): 32–40.

10. American Nurses Association, "Code of Ethics for Nurses with Interpretive Statements," accessed February 13, 2016, http://www.nursingworld.org/MainMenuCategories/EthicsStandards/CodeofEthicsforNurses/Code-of-Ethics-For-Nurses.html

11. Christine Grady, Marion Davis, Karen Soeken, Patricia O'Donnell, Carol Taylor, Adrienne Farrar and Connie Ulrich, "Does Nursing Education Influence the Moral Action of Practicing Nurses and Social Workers," *American Journal of Biomedical Ethics* 8, no. 4 (2008): 4–11.

12. Sharon Sousa, Ruth Griffin and Barbara Krainovich-Miller, "Professional Nursing Competence and Good Moral Character: A Policy Exemplar," *Journal of Nursing Law* 15, no. 2 (2012): 51–60.

13. Derek Sellman, "On Being of Good Character: Nurse Education and the Assessment of Good Character," *Nurse Education Today* 27 (2007): 765.

14. Nancy Crigger and Nelda Godfrey, "From the Inside Out: A New Approach to Teaching Professional Identity Formation and Professional Ethics," *Journal of Professional Nursing* 30, no. 5 (2014): 376–82.

15. Edie Braus, "Common Misconceptions About Professional Licensure," *American Journal of Nursing* 112, no. 10 (2012): 55–59.

16. Clare McCann, et al., "Resilience in the Health Professions: A Review of Recent Literature," *International Journal of Wellbeing* 3, no. 1 (2013): 60–81.

17. See Andrew Jameton, "Dilemmas of Moral Distress: Moral Responsibility and Nursing Practice," *AWHONNS Clinical Issues in Perinatal & Women's Health Nursing*, 4, no. 4 (1993): 542–51. See also, Elizabeth Epstein and Laura Delgado, "Understanding and Addressing Moral Distress," *Online Journal of Issues in Nursing* 15, no. 3 (2010): Manuscript 1.

Chapter Five

Effective Trustworthiness in the Professions

Trust has at least two enemies: "bad character and poor information."[1] While chapter 4 focused on the ways the professional community can work to develop good character on the part of its members, this chapter focuses on how professionals and professional communities communicate their posses- sion of trust warranting properties to trust-evaluators such as patients, clients, and the general public. When well communicated, trustworthiness becomes *effective trustworthiness.*

The unique features of the professional relationship make such signaling a challenge. As previously discussed, professionals often operate in relatively anonymous conditions in which others must make inferences about their trustworthiness with very limited amounts of information. In some cases, such as public administrators, professionals must secure the trust of a public with whom they have little to no personal interaction. How can trust be formed under such circumstances?

As in the development of trustworthiness itself, effective trustworthiness cannot be developed by the professional alone, but is the result of the con- certed effort of the profession working as an ethical community. The work of the ethical community not only develops the dispositional and instrumental trustworthiness of professionals, it also establishes a *reputation* for the pro- fessional role. Community members utilize this reputation as a resource when communicating their trustworthiness in relatively anonymous social conditions. However, reputation of the professional role alone is insufficient for effective trustworthiness. Professionals themselves must be adept at *sig- naling* their own trustworthiness to trust-evaluators. Such signaling is in- tended as an invitation to trust, and therefore creates implied promises on the part of the professionals that they can be relied upon to responsibly care for the interests of those who depend on them.

THE DEVELOPMENT OF PROFESSIONAL REPUTATION

Chapter 4 outlined a number of ways in which the professions work as ethical communities to promote trustworthiness on the part of its members. Professional communities:

- Support ongoing justificatory and application discourses that interpret the telos of the profession, determine the obligations and virtues that constitute competent professional practice, and how those virtues are best practiced in applied contexts.
- Use professional discourse to symbolically construct the "trustworthy professional" as a social type that practitioners are encouraged to internalize as part of their own sense of authenticity.
- Create discursive products, such as ethics codes, mission statements, white papers, and ethics opinions to articulate the demands of the professional role and give it discursive legitimacy in the minds of community members.
- Work to create educational environments that promote the development of moral competence and professional virtues.
- Create institutional environments, which lend practical credibility to the behavioral and dispositional demands of being a trustworthy professional.
- Develop and support disciplinary regimes that disincentivize misconduct.

Understood *internally*, the work of the professional community is aimed at developing the incentives and dispositions that make professionals trustworthy understood *externally*; many of these same practices are intended to promote the reputation of the professional role. For instance, when a profession supports an ongoing and rigorous ethico-moral discourse, it indicates to the public the priority it places on the ethical and moral dimensions of its practice. This increases the confidence of trust evaluators that members of the professional community possess trust-warranting properties.

These internal/external perspectives can be seen in a professional code of ethics. As a communicative gesture oriented internally to the community, the code is the concretization of the community's discourse on the appropriate principles, virtues, and conduct relative to the professional practice. In articulating the expectations community members have of one another, the ethics code serves as a basis for the "conventional" relationship among those community members.[2] Understood as externally-oriented communication, a code of ethics is an articulation of the commitments the members of professional communities make to clients and the public at large. As communicated externally, codes of ethics are *assurances* that members of a professional community can be relied upon to responsibly care for the interests entrusted to them; that is, that they are trustworthy.

Codes of ethics are not the only communicative gesture that professional communities make to create assurances of their trustworthiness. Professional associations and institutions (e.g., hospitals, firms, courts) offer a variety of communicative products aimed at assuring clients and the public of professional trustworthiness. Mission statements, ethics opinions, white papers, and even advertising are offered as assurances of the trustworthiness of the members of the professional community. However, such assurances are only as persuasive as the reputation of the professional community itself. The professions, therefore, have good reason to conduct community institutions in a way that promotes the reputation of the community itself. By maintaining a robust ethico-moral discourse; by developing professional virtues through training programs; by disciplining unethical community members; and by promoting social justice in their area of professional expertise; professional communities demonstrate to the public and would-be clients that the symbolic articulation of the "trustworthy professional" is not mere window dressing, but represents the genuine character and commitments of members of the professional community. When professional communities enjoy strong reputations, they are more effective at assuring trust evaluators that bona fide professional role-players are worthy of their trust.

As in the development of trustworthy professionals, professional associations play an important role in developing for the members of a profession a reputation for trustworthiness. Professional associations wield significant discursive and institutional power and are viewed by the public as the de facto representatives of the professional community. It is typically those professional associations that develop codes of ethics, issue ethics opinions, and generally support the ongoing ethico-moral discourse within the profession. They also work with educational institutions to develop appropriate standards of professional training, and with regulatory agencies in developing appropriate licensing and disciplinary standards. Professional associations also participate in the broader public discourse and contribute to the public deliberation on issues within professional areas of expertise. In this sense, professional associations offer their collective expert assistance to the public in order to create a more efficient and just society. When professional associations participate in public discourse as impartial contributors of expertise oriented toward efficiency and justice, they promote the reputation of the professional community as a whole.

When such reputations are successfully constructed, the public (including would-be clients) views members of the professional community as honest, diligent, discreet, loyal, and beneficent—at least relative to their professional practice. This reputation serves as an important warrant for anonymous trust in professionals.

Credentialing

Successful professional communities are able to develop their own reputation as communities committed to ethical professional practice. They can then use this reputational power as social capital to develop and lend credibility to the generic professional role-occupier as a practitioner with the requisite skills, knowledge base, and dispositions that make them worthy of trust. Through the process of *credentialing,* professional communities are able to transfer this social capital to individual professionals.

In many professions the process of credentialing is elaborate and involves the coordinated efforts of the professional community and state regulatory agencies. In licensed, "formal" professions such as law, medicine, and education, being a credentialed professional is a multitiered process. Professionals must be trained in educational programs certified by key professional associations working with state regulatory agencies. They then must successfully earn their professional degree, which in professions such as nursing and education, requires not only education in the requisite skills and knowledge base of competent professional practice, but training and assessment of one's character dispositions and moral competence. When professionals successfully complete their educational training, they are certified by their educational institution, and by extension by the professional community, to have the requisite skills, knowledge base, moral competence, and dispositions necessary for competent practice.

Simply having a degree from a recognized professional education program provides a certain measure of community credentialing to individual professionals. In the licensed professions, however, this is but the first step in the process. Profession-candidates must then seek the full certification of the professional community and the state by satisfying varying professional admission and licensing requirements.

Typically, licensed professionals must pass proficiency exams created and/or administered by key professional organizations. For instance, those aspiring to become Certified Public Accountants must take the Uniform CPA exam, which is developed by a key professional association, the American Institute of Certified Professional Accountants. In many states, CPA candidates must also take a professional ethics exam—designed either by the AICPA or by the state's professional association of CPAs.

In accounting, completing the proper course of education and passing the exams are necessary elements to becoming certified by the profession. To become "licensed" requires this professional endorsement as well as other requirements that state licensing boards—again often working closely with professional organizations—determine to be necessary to provide legal protections to the public. In the case of accounting, education and exams but are two of the three "E's." The last, "experience" is required by many state-licensing boards, and involves a certain amount of time working in accounting practice.

In licensed professions, being credentialed by the professional community and securing licensing from the state allows for the transference of the general reputation of the professional role to the individual practitioner. For professions that have successfully developed a reputation for trustworthiness for the generic role, credentialed professionals will enjoy the benefits of this reputation as well. Reputations establish an interpretive horizon by which the public understands the nature of the professional role. This creates a series of expectations that the public holds about the skills, knowledge, attitudes, and dispositions of anonymous professional role-players.

By developing and effectively communicating the reputation of the professional role, professional communities can "prime" the trusting expectations of the public. When the anonymous doctor walks through the door, the patient is already disposed to trust this particular role-player because of the reputation of the physician-as-social-type—a reputation developed and promoted by the medical community.

FROM REPUTATION TO INTERPERSONAL SIGNALING

The establishment of a professional reputation for trustworthiness is a boot-strapping mechanism that allows clients, patients, employers, and the general public to form anonymous trust based on the inference that those who occupy professional roles possess trust warranting properties. Trust evaluators rely on reputation to develop prima facie trust with professionals, but reputation alone is insufficient to develop robust and sustainable trust for a number of reasons. Most professions have been rocked by scandal over the last few decades and few, if any, still enjoy reputations by which credentialing alone is enough to guarantee trust. Patients are routinely aware of the conflicts of interest that face doctors, particularly in managed health-care settings; lawyers are widely perceived to be unscrupulous; and scandals in accounting have diminished the once sterling reputation of that profession as well. Even ministry, the only profession that has the luxury of enlisting God to burnish its reputation, has suffered from scandals that have badly damaged the perceived trustworthiness of the generic minister.

Moreover, while the training and credentialing of professionals can create a certain measure of assurance to the public that professional role holders are competent and trustworthy, it simply cannot guarantee that all professional role holders are such. The simple fact of the matter is that, despite rigorous education, credentialing and, for some professions, licensing requirements, some professionals are incompetent or unethical—or both. Again recent scandals have highlighted this for the public. As a result, while a good reputation for a particular professional role will likely incline someone to extend prima facie trust to a professional role-player, rational agents will also look for cues and assurances from any particular professional that he or she is trustworthy.

To successfully offer interpersonal assurances, effective signaling on the part of the professional is a necessary element in the development of trust. In economics and social psychology, *signaling theory* explores the ways in which trust-candidates can communicate their trustworthiness to trust-evaluators. Such signaling is generally necessary because trustworthiness is at least partly dispositional, yet dispositions are not readily apparent to those who must evaluate the trustworthiness of a trust-candidate.

A trust-candidate might possess the kind of character that makes him or her worthy of trust, but such character is not, in itself, immediately manifest to evaluators with little personal experience with the trust-candidate. Is the trust-candidate honest, diligent, or discreet? Those dispositional states essential to trustworthiness, but not immediately manifest to evaluators are termed *krypton* in signaling theory.[3] The challenge for trust-candidates such as professionals is to find ways to make their krypton manifest through the presentation of their social self.

The idea of a "presentation of the social self" is most famously associated with the ethnography of Erving Goffman who emphasized the role of *dramaturgical* action in which actors carefully "play" social roles in order to manage the impressions they create on their audience.[4] "Impression management" is sometimes criticized as a cynical view of social interaction, but it need not be so. Good professionals, for instance, have powerful reasons to develop trust with would-be clients, patients, employers, and members of the public. Because developing such trust requires not only having certain dispositions, but also effectively communicating the possession of those dispositions, professions have good reasons to carefully manage the impressions they make on their audience.[5]

In cases in which the professional role itself enjoys a reputation for trustworthiness, professionals can exploit signals that link their identity to that of the trusted social type. "Identity" signaling aims at providing the right kind of "signature" which can transfer the primed expectations on the part of the public to the particular professional practitioner. One kind of signaling used in creating trust aims to show that the professional is a bona fide member of the professional community, and that the inferences the trust-evaluator makes about the generic professional role-player, are valid for the particular professional role-player. Professionals routinely display diplomas and other certificates indicating their formal credentials and licenses.

Professionals must also carefully "play the role" of the relevant social type by adhering to the kinds of cues, habits, and styles expected of the social role. In many, if not most professions this means signaling trustworthiness by means of manners of dress, speech, and overall presentation of the physical self. For instance, in the early to mid-twentieth century there were few female lawyers in the United States, and those few practicing female lawyers were frequently mistaken for legal secretaries. To combat this, a number of prominent female attorneys began wearing distinctive large brimmed hats as a signal that distinguished them as lawyers. The practice caught on and became an effective means by which women attorneys could signal their bona fides as professional role-players.

By successfully signaling one's identity (e.g., doctor, nurse, lawyer, engineer), professionals can make use of the reputation of their professional role to bootstrap their way to developing trust with client, patients, and other dependents. However, even effective signaling of one's social type cannot assure the development of trust. While reputations are important bootstrapping mechanisms, trust evaluators are keenly aware that reputations are but generalizations and do not guarantee that the professional before them will exhibit the dispositions of the reputed role-player.

Signaling one's trustworthiness requires going beyond social-type identity signatures. Professionals also need to signal their *personal* trust worthiness. The variety of physical and interpersonal signals made by the professional can be offered as authenticity signals to trust evaluators that the particular professional is genuinely trustworthy. The professional's tone of voice, facial expressions, eye contact, body posture, and presence in the moment can all be effective signals to trust evaluators that this particular role-player possesses relevant trust-warranting properties.

A visit to any doctor's office demonstrates identity and authenticity signaling at work. A doctor's office is an ethnic domain saturated with signals aimed at promoting the trust of the patient. The office is fundamentally divided between, as Goffman puts it, "frontstage" and "backstage"[6] areas that allow for the controlled presentation of the doctor and his or her staff. The main front stage is the waiting room, and it is here that important first impressions are made on the patient. For this reason, such rooms are designed to be comfortable and soothing. Importantly, a good waiting room is large enough so that flow of waiting patients does not crowd it. A long wait in a crowded waiting room signals inefficiency, incompetence, and a lack of care on the part of the physician. To manage this impression, physicians make use of multiple examination rooms to increase efficiency and manage patient flow.[7] When the process is well designed, patients flow quickly from the waiting area to an examination room where they begin their interactions with a nurse. By locating examination rooms "backstage," physicians signal the esoteric nature of medical expertise. By "allowing" patients backstage, the patient experiences a departure from everyday life and an entry into the "world" of medicine.

The examination room itself replicates the front stage/backstage bifurcation. The examination room is filled with identity signals of the physicians' credentials such as diplomas, board certificates, medical diagrams, and other informational literature. Physicians subtly communicate their commitment to discretion by making examination rooms reasonably soundproof and with doors that open in toward examination rooms rather than out into hallways. While the patient waits in the examination room, taking in the variety of identity and authenticity signals of trustworthiness, the physician is in yet another backstage area not authorized for the patient's observation. This could be other examination rooms, a procedure room, or the doctor's private office. The doctor finally arrives, sweeping on to the stage in the professional "costume": lab coat, professional attire, and the ubiquitous stethoscope.

The physician can then offer authenticity signals of his or her personal trustworthiness by interacting with the patient in an empathetic and respectful manner. The physician's tone of voice, eye contact, body language, and word choice are all subtle signals that trust-evaluators will use in making a swift inference as to this particular physician's trustworthiness. Physicians also signal their trustworthiness in the way communication with patients is structured. For instance, they signal their respect for patient autonomy through open and transparent communication aimed at joint decision making.

By creating an ethnic domain that signals a commitment to medical expertise, efficiency, privacy, safety, economy, convention, and comfort, the physician makes clear to patients that he or she is a typical member of the medical community and that the good reputation enjoyed by physicians generally is also well placed in this particular physician. Moreover, the authenticity signals presented in the office space demonstrate to the patient the physician's specific dispositional trustworthiness—that he or she is committed to *caring* for the patient in a competent, discreet, and efficient manner.

Secondary Trust: Signals and Charlatans

The primary problem for trust evaluators is determining whether a particular agent's dispositions make him or her worthy of trust. This problem is resolved by making such krypta manifest to trust evaluators via effective signaling. This gives rise, however, to a secondary problem for trust evaluators, who additionally need to assess which signals are *reliable* indicators of the trustworthiness of an agent's dispositions given the possibility of charlatans. [8] For instance, certain facial expressions, tones of voice, and eye contact can be signals of dispositional honesty. In ordinary interactions trust evaluators routinely appeal to such signs when "sizing up" trust-candidates. The problem with such signs, however, is that they are relatively costless and easily mimicked by opportunists in an effort to deceive trust-evaluators. As a result, the higher the risk entailed by the interaction, the more demanding the rational trust evaluator will be in assessing the signals of an agent's trustworthiness.

When signaling to patients, clients, and other potential dependents, professions therefore have good reasons to use signals that would be relatively costly for opportunists to mimic. For instance, when a UPS employee arrives at a home to deliver a package, most people hardly give the authenticity of the employee a second thought.[9] Securing a large truck, painting it brown with a UPS logo, and purchasing a UPS uniform are all costly endeavors. As a result, when an individual wearing a UPS uniform pulls up in a large brown truck with a UPS logo emblazoned on it, most trust evaluators take these as reliable signs that the individual is, in fact, a UPS employee and can be trusted to deliver a package.

Importantly, not only would securing such a vehicle and uniform be costly, but also in an effective legal system that enforces trademarks, charlatans run the risk of legal punishment simply in making such signals. On the other hand, if someone pulls up to a residence in an unmarked white van with no uniform claiming to be selling steaks from the local butcher shop (which has happened to the author!), rational agents generally would be wise to withhold their trust. Of course, such judgments are contextual. If one is a guard at a high security prison, one might find a brown truck with a UPS logo to be insufficient to warrant trust. Likewise, if there has been a rash of robberies by UPS impersonators, then signals such as logos and uniforms will cease to be effective.

To assure would-be clients, patients, and other dependents that they are bona fide trustworthy professionals, the most efficient signaling used by professionals is one that is costly for charlatans to mimic. The physician's office is an elaborate set-up in which numerous details—furniture, office space, physical arrangement, decor and displays of credentials—would be costly to duplicate. Moreover, professional credentials and licensing are typically very costly to obtain and involve rigorous confirmation procedures. For this reason, it is very difficult and costly for charlatans to secure such credentials. Of course, a charlatan could simply print and display bogus degrees, credentials and licenses, but in an effective legal system that bans such mimicry, charlatans take on the cost of legal sanctions by their bogus signaling.

A professional trust-candidate might be a charlatan in a second sense. He or she could legitimately possess the proper credentials and licensing, but fail to be personally trustworthy. While most doctors, nurses, engineers and even lawyers are ethical, there are of course many professionals who lack trust-warranting properties. For this reason, while professional ethics should not be understood as simply creating external inducements to comply with a set of rules of conduct, disciplinary mechanisms on the part of professional communities and state licensing agencies are, nonetheless, an important part of the trust building process. Identity signals communicate to trust-evaluators that the professional is a bona fide member of the profession. From this membership, trust-evaluators can infer a certain measure of instrumental trustworthiness insofar as credentialed and licensed professionals have powerful incentives to avoid serious misconduct. In other words, disciplinary schemes make it costly for professionals to mimic personal trustworthiness.

FROM SIGNALING TO ETHICAL ACTION

Effectively communicating a professional's trustworthiness requires not only the development of a positive community reputation, but also the appropriate signaling that links the particular practitioner with that reputation. The most effective signal of one's trustworthiness comes from the ethical nature of one's *conduct*.[10] Treating patients, clients, and other dependents in ways that are honest, beneficent, discreet, diligent, and respectful of autonomy is the best indication that the professional actually possesses those dispositions. Reputation and signal management can help "bootstrap" trust so that trust-evaluators are willing to form prima facie trust. However, if the professional's actual conduct indicates that he or she lacks trustworthy dispositions, the robust levels of trust needed for effective professional practice quickly will evaporate.

When professionals act in ways that are deceptive, paternalistic, unfair, or manipulative, trust evaluators withdraw trust and adopt a variety of hedging strategies that limit their vulnerability, but also make professional practice much less effective.[11] Indeed, if the impression management by the professional is perceived to be manipulative window dressing, it backfires and drains trust from the relationship. To overcome these problems, it is essential that impression management be understood within a broader, nonstrategic action context in which clients, patients, and other dependents are treated in ways consistent with the trustworthy dispositions that professionals claim to possess. Here Jürgen Habermas's idea of "communicative action" is helpful.

The idea of communicative action is best understood in contrast with "strategic" action. In strategic action agents are not interested in mutual understanding or intersubjective evaluation of their goals and the means to attain them. They are interested instead in efficiently achieving their goals, and treat others as objective elements of the world that may be utilized in order to achieve their ends. In strategic action, those with whom one interacts are not intrinsically valuable, nor are the relationships one maintains with them. They are only valuable insofar as they promote the achievement of one's interests.

In contrast, communicative action is a "second-person standpoint," grounded on an "I-Thou" participant stance, mediated through communication, toward mutual understanding, intersubjective evaluation, and consensus. Communicative action begins with the practical commitment that the other is an inherently valuable member of one's moral community to whom one owes rational accountability. Understood this way, goals are adopted as *joint* goals. When pursuing joint goals, communicative actors are committed to intersubjective evaluation of both the worthiness of those goals and the appropriate means to achieve them. [12]

Communicative action creates a context in which professionals are able to put their virtues to work. In recognizing the client as a "Thou" with inherent dignity, professionals commit themselves to treating the client with honesty, beneficence, discretion, and in ways that respects his or her autonomy. Treating clients virtuously in the context of communicative action creates real substance that supports the signals of one's trustworthiness.

When engaging in communicative action, professionals create deliberative, transparent, and symmetrical forms of communication in which clients (or the public) are genuine participants in dialogue oriented toward consensus. This promotes the exercise of the professional virtues by creating a favorable action context for honesty, respect for autonomy, beneficence, and loyalty. Compare this with strategic action, in which the client (or public) is considered an object to be processed. Such a standpoint, even if motivated by beneficence as in traditional medicine, promotes paternalism, deception, and disregard for client autonomy.

Dramaturgical action—that is, action as performance aimed at creating certain impressions—is often criticized for being a form of strategic manipulation. However, by integrating dramaturgical and communicative action, the effectively trustworthy professional is better able to create trusting relationships with clients and the general public. Far from being manipulative, professionals are morally obligated to create such relationships, and consequently have good reasons to engage in impression management. By doing so within a framework of communicative action, virtuous professionals both signal their trustworthiness and create an action context favorable for honoring the trust they have invited from clients, patients, and the public. When professionals honor that trust through virtuous professional practice, they promote even more robust forms of trust from those who depend on them.

FROM ETHICAL ACTION BACK TO REPUTATION

This chapter began with a consideration of the role of the professional community in developing a robust reputation for the professional as social-type. Reputational development by the professional community serves as an important bootstrapping measure by which trust-evaluators can build prima facie trust with professionals. This allows the impression management of the individual professional to develop the richer levels of trust necessary for effective professional practice. This trust is reinforced by the professional's demonstration of trustworthiness through virtuous behavior in the context of communicative action. In honoring the trust of those who depend on them, professionals not only enhance that trust, they also promote the generalized reputation of their social role—with the end result of promoting the effective trustworthiness of their profession generally.

When making generalizations of social types, an important—and for some researchers on trust, *the most important*—evidence for trust evaluators is their experiences with previous individuals of that type. Behavior by a physician that indicates untrustworthiness makes a patient less likely to trust *physicians generally.* There is, then, an important interactive, and mutually reinforcing, relationship between the reputation of a social role and the conduct of individuals who play that role. For this reason the effective trustworthiness of a given professional must work in two distinct social dimensions.

At the community level, the profession works to create the kind of symbolic identity, training, and credentialing standards that produce genuinely trustworthy professionals. Professional communities also use these efforts to promote the reputation of the professional role or social-type. At the individual level, each professional can utilize the reputation of the professional role by signaling his or her authorized occupation of that role. Professionals also use interpersonal signaling to communicate their personal possession of trust-warranting properties. Finally, the substantive ethical and moral quality of professional conduct itself has a feedback effect on the reputation of their professional role.

There is a common expression in mountaineering to the effect that when climbers rope themselves to one another, they are both promoting their safety *and forming a suicide pact.* Like roped climbers, members of a profession are "in it together" when it comes to building trust with patients, clients, and other dependents. The conduct of unscrupulous professionals has a negative effect on the reputation needed by all members of the profession in offering their effective expert assistance. Professional misconduct leads trust-evaluators to infer that the professional social-type is not trustworthy, and that the signals given by the professional community and the individual professionals are but manipulative window dressing.

The interconnectedness of professionals in maintaining the reputation essential for effective trustworthiness provides yet another reason for professionals, as members of the professional community, to adopt the authenticity paradigm of professional ethics that aims to develop the virtues necessary for individuals to be trustworthy professionals. For, as it turns out, clients, patients, and the public are not the only people placed at risk by the potential misconduct of professionals. Fellow professionals themselves are also at risk. When a teacher sexually abuses a student, *all* teachers are harmed. When a physician harms a patient in pursuit of profit, all physicians are harmed. When a lawyer deceives a client, all lawyers are harmed. For this reason, professional communities have good reason to promote and demand standards of conduct for all professional-role holders, and to create disciplinary schemes aimed at deterring unethical conduct and removing unscrupulous professionals.

Less dramatically, even ethical professionals can damage the reputation of their professional role through poor impression management. For example, a teacher who poorly signals his or her trustworthiness to parents produces mistrust that extends beyond the immediate relationship at hand. Because interaction with individuals from social-types is important evidence used in forming generalizations about those types, these parents will likely revise their overall impression of teachers *generally*—thereby damaging the reputation of the professional-role itself. For this reason, professional communities have good reason to promote and demand standards of impression management on the part of community members. In teacher education programs, for instance, training and assessment of "professional dispositions" include not only the professional virtues, but also dispositions to *present oneself* in ways that effectively signal trustworthiness.

SIGNALS, ASSURANCES, AND PROMISES

In the development of the reputation of the professional role as well as the identity and authenticity signaling of professional practitioners, trust evaluators are assured that professionals possess trust-warranting properties and can therefore be relied upon to exercise the professional virtues in the responsible care of the interests entrusted to them. In making such assurances, professionals, as members of communities, and as individuals, make a commitment to those they serve—a commitment that some commentators have argued amounts to promising. Others have argued that while some the explicit assurances offered by professionals, such as oaths, are promises, it strains the idea of promising to think of general signaling of professional trustworthiness as constituting promises.

Promises are fascinating moral and social phenomena. In promising, one creates special obligations that previously did not exist. Identifying the source of promissory obligations has been a vexing problem in ethics. How is it that merely adding, "I promise" to a particular statement generates a moral duty? The traditional answer to this question was to locate the duty in the idea of veracity. Breaking a promise is wrong, in this view, because it amounts to a lie. However, as David Hume and others pointed out, this simply will not do. Henry Sidgwick offers the paradigmatic objection here:

> If I merely assert my intention of abstaining from alcohol for a year, and then after a week take some, I am (at worst) ridiculed as inconsistent: but if I have pledged myself to abstain, I am blamed as *untrustworthy*. Thus the essential element of the Duty of Good Faith seems to be not conformity to my own statement, but to expectations that I have intentionally raised in others. [13] [emphasis added]

The key to promises is not a duty to veracity per se, but a duty to honor the trust invited from others. [14] When one breaks a promise, one engages in a kind of *manipulation* of the promisee's vulnerability—a manipulation which reasonable persons have good reasons to refuse permission to others. Understood in terms of trust, a promise then can be understood as:

1. a communication made by a promisor which
2. invites a promisee to assume a certain vulnerability to the promisor
3. in light of:

    a. the promisor's firm intention to perform action X; and

    b. the promisor's recognition that absent special circumstances, the promisee's trust obligates the performance of X (provided that the promisor is morally free to do so)

The obligation created by a promise is a strict obligation of fidelity, one that is typically waived only if promisor is not morally free to X, or the promisee has released the promisor from the promise.

A professional oath is clearly a promise, as it invites the public and one's peers to trust the professional to engage in the accepted standards of conduct. As moral statements, oaths also make clear the professional's recognition that he or she is morally bound by the pledged standards of conduct. But aside from oaths, are the various forms of communication and signaling used by professionals to invite trust best understood as promises? A doctor wearing a stethoscope is a signal of the physician's trustworthiness and is an invitation to trust, but for many commentators it seems implausible to think of such signaling as "promising." One might think of such commitments instead in light of the legal doctrine of "implied contract."

Consider a stingy restaurant customer who refuses to pay for a meal because there was no binding agreement to do so. The menu, the customer argues, listed prices for food items, but did not state that the customer must actually pay those prices, and certainly did not state that the customer must pay at the conclusion of the meal. Thus he refuses to pay, or at best agrees to pay on Tuesday for the hamburger he ate today. The doctrine of implied contract holds that, even in the absence of an explicit agreement, the "totality of the circumstances" created an implied binding agreement to pay for the meal. A restaurant is a well-known social institution, and the social role "customer" is common and familiar. Provided that the restaurant followed the typical social conventions, the customer knew, or should have known, that as a "customer" at a "restaurant" there was an obligation to pay at the conclusion of the meal.

Professional roles function in the same way. Professional communities go to great lengths to create professional roles that are well known for their trustworthiness. Individual professionals, through oaths, codes of ethics, and other explicit forms of communication invite the trust of those who depend on them—they invite others to rely on them to responsibly care for the important interests of others. When professionals then signal their bona fide occupation of a professional role, and their dispositional trustworthiness, they personally invite individuals to rely on them to perform their role in the appropriate manner. The totality of these communications—from explicit oaths down to interpersonal signaling—creates an implied binding agreement on the part of the professional to properly perform his or her role.

Viewing professional role commitments as implied contracts is a valuable insight, but there are nonetheless good reasons to think of professional role commitments as implied promises as opposed to implied contracts. Contracts and promises are both binding agreements; however, contracts are morally weaker than promises in a number of important respects. Absent special circumstances, promisors are typically only released from fidelity by the consent of the promisee. This makes promises different from other types of agreements that can be dissolved via timely warning or compensation for loss.

If Travis promises Paola that he will wax her cross-country skis before the race on Saturday, then, absent special circumstances, he must do so. If he changes his mind on Wednesday, Paola can find him blameworthy. "But you promised!" she might rightfully object. Contracts, on the other hand, can be dissolved without the consent of the contractee. Provided timely warning is given and the contractee suffers no damages, breaching a contract is held harmless. Even more dramatically, breaching a contract is held harmless even when a contractor fails to honor the contract because a more profitable arrangement presented itself. Provided the contractor compensates the contractee for any loss suffered for nonperformance, the breach is held harmless.

The commitments made by professionals are not best understood as contracts because they are not waived so easily. Indeed, what is precisely communicated to clients and the public is a *zealous* commitment to honesty, loyalty, diligence, confidentiality, and respect for autonomy. For this reason, it would be inappropriate for a professional to expect release from, for instance, the duty of confidentiality, simply through timely warning and the expectation that the client will not be injured by the disclosure.

Professional duties are generally binding unless released by the client, or when the professional is not morally free (e.g., due to conflicting professional duties) to honor them. For this reason, the explicit and implicit assurances that professionals make as to their trustworthiness constitute an implied promise that they can be relied upon to conduct themselves in an ethical manner. Some of these promises are explicit, as in an oath, whereas others are implied by the totality of the circumstances created by the professional role and the signaling made by role-players.

CONCLUSION

For trustworthiness to be effective at developing trust, professional communities work to develop robust reputations for the professional social role, while individual practitioners utilize this reputation in their professional "signature" and buttress it with their authenticity signaling. The communication of one's trustworthiness in the professional context invites clients, employers, the public, and even professional peers, to trust the professional in light of the professional's commitment to ethical conduct. This commitment is expressed in a number of explicit promises, such as oaths and ethics codes, and is implied by the totality of the circumstances by when an individual presents him or herself as a professional.

The appearances created by professional conduct are by no means simply a matter of marketing or brand. Because professionals have moral and ethical reasons to be effectively trustworthy, the impression management of professionals is a matter of praise or blame. This has important consequences for a number of issues professional ethics, such as the nature and evaluation of "conflicts of interest." This will be explored in the next chapter.

NOTES

1. Michael Bacharach and Diego Gambetta, "Trust in Signs," in *Trust and Society*, 150.

2. Edmund Pellegrino, "The Medical Profession as a Moral Community," *Bulletin of the New York Academy of Medicine* 66, no. 3 (1990): 223.

3. Bacharach and Gambetta, "Trust in Signs," 154.

4. Erving Goffman, *The Presentation of the Self in Everyday Life* (New York: Doubleday, 1959).

5. James Chriss, "Habermas, Goffman and Communicative Action: Implications for Professional Practice," *American Sociological Review* 60 (1995): 545–65.

6. Goffman, 120–30.

7. Jon Wells, "Efficient Office Space for a Successful Practice," *Family Practice Management Journal* 14, no. 5, 2007: 46–50.

8. Bacharach and Gambetta, 158.

9. Bacharach and Gambetta, 161.

10. Bacharach and Gambetta, 165.

11. Tom Tyler, "Why Do People Rely on Others? Social Identity and Social Aspects of Trust," in *Trust in Society,* 285–307.

12. Jürgen Habermas, *Theory of Communicative Action,* trans. Thomas McCarthy (Boston: Beacon Press, 1984), 18.

13. Henry Sidgwick, *The Methods of Ethics* (London: MacMillan, 1907), 146.

14. For accounts of promising as an invitation to trust, see Nicholas Southwood and David Friedrich, "Promises Beyond Assurance," *Philosophical Studies* 144 (2009): 261–80. See also, Thomas Scanlon, "Promises and Practices," *Philosophy and Public Affairs* 19, no. 3 (1990): 199–226.

Chapter Six

Conflicts of Interest

The pain medication Vioxx was approved for market by the Food and Drug Administration in 1999 and was soon widely prescribed for patients struggling with arthritic pain. That same year, Merck, the manufacturer of the drug, launched the VIGOR study (Vioxx Gastrointestinal Outcomes Research) to determine if Vioxx produced fewer gastrointestinal side effects compared to naproxen—another popular nonsteroidal anti-inflammatory drug (NSAID). The study soon revealed that Vioxx produced fewer such side effects, but it also revealed that those taking Vioxx were suffering roughly *twice* as many cardiovascular events (e.g., heart attacks) compared to those in the naproxen group. Many experts later argued that at this point the safety committee charged with trial participant safety should have halted the trial. Curt Furberg, former head of clinical trials as the National Heart, Lung, and Blood Institute commented:

> A doubling in risk is quite remarkable. The committee, in my view, should have told the sponsor to stop the study and told the world this drug is harmful. Unfortunately that was not done, and I think that contributed to the tragedy with Vioxx. [1]

The committee charged with participant safety allowed the study to continue on the assumption that naproxen might have an "aspirin effect" which was reducing the incidence of cardiovascular events for the naproxen group. If true, then Vioxx was not increasing the incidence of cardiovascular events so much as naproxen was *decreasing* them. The problem with this "aspirin effect" hypothesis, however, was that there was there were no studies supporting the idea that naproxen possessed the aspirin effect necessary to explain the difference in cardiovascular events between the naproxen group and the Vioxx group. Later, a Merck researcher would refer to the hypothesis as "wishful thinking."[2]

Not only did the participant safety committee allow the study to continue based on a dubious hypothesis, its chairperson, Dr. Michael Weinblatt, agreed—at Merck's suggestion—to end the reporting of data from the trial before the effects of the drug would have presented in some patients—indeed before some patients would even leave the study.[3] As a result, when the results of the VIGOR trial were published in the *New England Journal of Medicine*, the rate of cardiovascular events for the Vioxx group was underreported.[4]

Concerns about increased cardiovascular events associated with Vioxx did not stay buried for long. By 2001 the FDA Arthritis Advisory Committee reviewed the complete VIGOR data and concluded there was a significant increased risk of cardiovascular events associated with Vioxx.[5] Later that year, *The New York Times* published an article raising concerns about Vioxx's safety.[6] The evidence of the dangers of Vioxx continued to mount and in 2004, five years after the VIGOR study, Merck took Vioxx off the market. By then millions of Americans had taken the drug, and an analysis by the British medical journal *Lancet* estimated that 88,000 of them had suffered cardiovascular events attributable to Vioxx, of which some 35,000 had died.[7]

Why had the VIGOR participant safety committee allowed the study to continue? Why did it appeal to a dubious "aspirin effect" hypothesis in the absence of scientific evidence? Why had it not raised public concern about Vioxx? Why did it allow data to be collected from the study in a way that underreported the risks associated with Vioxx? The answers to these questions may never be known with certainty, but the simple fact of the matter is that Merck was depending on the popular drug to create a robust revenue stream for the company, and was therefore keen to minimize any damaging effect the trial could create for Vioxx's marketability. Did this affect the judgment of the participant safety committee? There is good reason to think that it did.

Dr. Weinblatt, while chairing the safety committee also owned (with his wife) over $70,000 of Merck stock. Even worse, documents produced in the lawsuits regarding Vioxx showed that in February 2000, during the very time those critical negotiations on how to collect the VIGOR data were taking place, Weinblatt was offered and accepted a consultant position with Merck. The position would entail twelve days of work over a two-year period at a rate of $5,000 per day.[8] Weinblatt signed the contract shortly after the conclusion of the VIGOR trial. By doing so, he narrowly avoided conflict of interest regulations. Critics later decried Weinblatt's conflict of interest, a conflict that he denied because, in his view, he never placed his personal interests ahead of his duties to protect the safety of the VIGOR participants.[9]

The Vioxx case is but one of a myriad of scandals that have rocked the professions in the last few decades. "Conflict of interest"—a concept that hardly existed fifty years ago—is now widely recognized as a major cause of professional misconduct. But as Weinblatt's defense indicates, there is much debate about what constitutes a conflict of interest, when such conflicts are morally blameworthy, and how they should best be managed.

In this chapter, a "conflict of interest" is defined and assessed in light of the professional's obligation to be effectively trustworthy. Conflicts of interest are undesirable because they diminish the instrumental, dispositional and effective trustworthiness of professionals. When professionals voluntarily practice with avoidable conflicts of interest—as did Weinblatt—they are morally blameworthy. However, unavoidable conflicts can also be damaging to professional trustworthiness and need to be responsibly managed. Finally, conflicts of interest are not only an issue for individual practitioners, but can affect professional associations as well. Given the importance of professional associations as anchors of the profession as an ethical community, "organizational" conflict of interest is also morally problematic.

WHAT IS A CONFLICT OF INTEREST?

Professionals can be thought of as having *primary* and *secondary* interests.[10] As previously discussed, professionals qua professionals, have an interest in promoting the essential or internal goods of the professional practice in light of its overall constitutive end or telos. In medicine, such internal goods include the health and alleviation of suffering on the part of patients; in engineering, they include efficiency and safety of design; in education, they include the development of the intellectual and character virtues of the student. Those who rely on professionals entrust them with important interests related to the professional telos. Part of the primary interests of professionals qua professionals is therefore to honor that trust and responsibly care for those interests.

Professionals have a variety of other interests as well, with perhaps the most influential being profit, prestige, power, and personal relationships. These interests are by no means illegitimate. While the professions are guided by a service ideal, working as a professional is not volunteerism. Professionals are compensated in both financial and cultural capital, and because of their expertise they are often in a position to reap significant financial and reputational rewards for their work. Less glamorously, but no less importantly, professionals are ordinary human beings who depend on their professional income in supporting themselves and their families. Professional practice can also come with significant power. Doctors, lawyers, judges, and teachers have power over others, power that grows as one advances in one's career. It is not surprising that flourishing professionals will seek out the opportunities and responsibilities that come from increased power. Finally, professional practice is a social practice, so professionals have a valid interest in developing relationships with peers and with the community more broadly. Professionals are also ordinary people with families and friends and wish to see their loved ones do well.

While profit, prestige, power, and personal relationships are valid interests, they are nonetheless *secondary* from a professional perspective in at least two respects. Teleologically, these interests are not essential or intrinsic to the professional practice. An individual who maliciously harms patients can very reasonably be thought as failing to be a "true" physician. The nature of the role "physician" is, by its very nature, incompatible with such harms. On the other hand, interests such as profit are not internal or essential to the nature of the profession. A physician who volunteers his or her time with Doctors Without Borders may not make money doing so, but is still very much a "true" physician.

Profit, prestige, power, and personal relationships are also secondary interests in a normative sense relative to the obligations and virtues of the professional. Because they invite trust, and hence vulnerability, professionals have an obligation to honor that trust by responsibly caring for the client's or patient's interests. Dispositionally trustworthy professionals take that dependence as a compelling and motivationally efficacious reason to responsibly care for the client's interest. *Loyal* professionals give priority to the client's interests over their own, and in doing so, make those interests *primary.*

Ideally there is an alignment or harmony between the professional's primary and secondary interests. Serving clients well is good for business. Satisfied clients and patients are more likely to return, and more likely to recommend the professional to others, which in turn burnishes the reputation of the individual professional and the profession itself. That increased prestige is often the basis for increased professional power. However, there are a variety of practical arrangements in which the professional's primary and secondary interests are not well aligned. Blatant cases such as bribery and nepotism show that otherwise valid secondary interests can come into conflict with performance of one's professional duties. When the secondary interests of the professional are such that they pose a serious threat to the promotion of primary interests the profession can be said to have a *conflict of interest.* Howard Brody argues that a conflict of interest exists when:

1. A professional has a fiduciary duty to promote the relevant (primary) interests of a trustor (e.g., client, patient, the public).

2. The professional is also subject to *secondary* interests. These could be their own immediate interests, or the interests of a third party.

3. The professional practices in an action context arranged in such a way that a reasonable observer would infer that a professional of normal psychology would be tempted to neglect the primary interests and instead prioritize secondary interests. [11]

For example, while technically avoiding the legal regulations at the time, Dr. Weinblatt's situation in the Vioxx case was, by this account, a conflict of interest. As a physician and chairperson of the VIGOR safety committee, his primary interest was to protect the health of the VIGOR participants and the public. Being a holder of a significant amount of stock, and as a soon-to-be consultant for Merck, he had an economic interest in promoting the well-being of the company. As a physician, his obligation to the participants was primary, while his economic interest in Merck was secondary. However, the situation was clearly one that a reasonable observer would conclude that a professional of normal psychology would be tempted to prioritize secondary interests at the expense of primary ones. As one expert put it, "it looks as though the [safety committee] could not have been reliable, and certainly as a patient myself, I would not have trusted it, and I would have objected profoundly to these arrangements." [12]

Such objections would have been quite reasonable because it appears that in the Vioxx case secondary interests carried the day. Merck, who did not want the VIGOR trial halted, insisted that data from the trial be collected in ways that would minimize evidence about the dangers of Vioxx. Both of those things came to pass in large measure because of the choices made by Dr. Weinblatt.

Merck also aggressively marketed Vioxx and used gift giving, edu-vacations, and other inducements to create financial incentives for physicians to prescribe the drug. Merck also used techniques to build personal relationships between pharmaceutical representatives ("drug reps") and physicians. These relationships became important in the process of "detailing" in which the drug rep, who often had no scientific background, would explain to the physician the benefits and risks of drugs such as Vioxx. The more reps could cultivate their relationships with physicians, the more they could push Vioxx and calm physician fears about the emerging literature on its risks.

ASSESSING CONFLICTS OF INTEREST

Some professionals and ethicists argue that conflicts of interest, while perhaps undesirable, are not morally blameworthy in and of themselves. Rather, they are "red flags" that call for increased vigilance, but not blame and prohibition. However, given the obligation for professionals to be effectively trustworthy, even in the absence of malfeasance, practicing under certain conflicts of interest is morally blameworthy. [13]

As has been argued in previous sections of this book, particularly in chapter 2, professionals have an obligation to invite and develop the trust of those they intend to serve. By extension they have an obligation to be *trustworthy*; that is, they should possess trust-warranting properties such as professional virtues (depositional trustworthiness), and aligned primary and secondary interests (instrumental trustworthiness). To invite and develop trust, professionals must also be *effectively trustworthy* in that they effectively communicate their trustworthiness to clients, patients, and the general public. Conflicts of interest are undesirable, and sometimes blameworthy, because they undermine the effective trustworthiness of the professional by making it more likely that he or she will fail to responsibly care for the primary interests entrusted to them. In other words, conflicts of interest make professionals less trustworthy both instrumentally and dispositionally. Conflicts of interest also undermine the effective communication of the professional's trustworthiness by creating the impression that the professional is, or will be, unreliable. This is especially the case when the professional operates with an *avoidable* conflict of interest. In such cases, the professional signals to trust evaluators an indifference to the risks posed by such temptations.

Instrumental Trustworthiness and Conflict of Interest

A professional is *instrumentally* trustworthy if and only if it is in his or her self-interest to responsibly care for the vulnerability of those they serve. In such cases, one can say the interests of the professional "encapsulate" those of the client or patient. For this reason, when the primary and secondary interests of the profession become misaligned, professionals are, *by definition*, less instrumentally trustworthy. When the misaligned secondary interests are powerful enough that they would create a significant temptation for a person with normal psychology to neglect the primary interests, the conflict represents a genuine threat to the performance of the professional's duties.

For rational trust evaluators a conflict of interest on the part of the professional counts as a powerful reason to adopt a variety of hedging strategies, and perhaps even withholding trust altogether. Professionals have good reasons to avoid the kinds of arrangements that encourage hedging on the part of those who depend on them because such strategies significantly limit the effectiveness of professional service—service that they have promised to provide.

Dispositional Trustworthiness and Conflict of Interest

While interest encapsulation is an important element of trustworthiness, it is not the only source of a professional's fiduciary reliability. Professionals can also be trustworthy because of virtuous dispositions that are well entrenched in their character. Virtuous professionals possess character traits that promote the achievement of the internal or essential goods of their professional practice. Such virtues include loyalty, beneficence, honesty, and respect for autonomy, discretion, diligence, integrity, and resilience. These virtues provide stable motivations for professionals to take the trusting dependence of clients and the like as an efficacious reason to responsibly care for the interests entrusted to them. The structural virtues of integrity and resilience provide motivation to remain steadfast in one's commitments even in the face of adversity.

Professionals who object to being criticized for having a conflict of interest often appeal to their dispositional trustworthiness as a reason why such conflicts are merely "apparent" and not real. It also explains why such professionals take the claim that they are conflicted as an affront. After all, virtuous professionals are motivated not by self-interest, no matter how powerful the incentives, but by their loyalty to those they serve. One might conclude that to find a professional's conflict of interest morally objectionable is to infer that the professional lacks virtues such as loyalty and integrity.

Conflicts of interest do, however, have a diminishing effect on the dispositional trustworthiness of professionals. While character virtues are stable personality traits, few people, if any, possess them perfectly. As a result, the possession of the virtues typically results in stable *tendencies* of principled action. However, even decent people, under the right conditions and presented with the right incentives, can suffer from what the Ancient Greeks called *akrasia*—a weakness of will in which the motivational foundation of the virtue is temporarily dissolved by other incentives. These incentives, usually the attainment of short-term goals, can render even a reasonably good person like (as Aristotle puts it) a "drunk mathematician" who has temporarily lost his or her otherwise stable ability to do advanced geometry.[14] Even the virtuous are not entirely immune from the effects of incentivized vice.

For this reason, conflicts of interest are a genuine threat to the reliability of even the otherwise dispositionally trustworthy professional. Situations that increase the incentives for professionals to fail in their fiduciary duties put more pressure on the professional's character—and most people have a breaking point in which temptation overwhelms what Lincoln called "the better angels of our nature." All things being equal, the professional with a conflict of interest is less likely to be dispositionally trustworthy than one free of such conflicts.

The threat posed by conflicts of interest to a professional's dispositional trustworthiness will motivate virtuous professionals to avoid them because possessing a virtue is to place great *value* on it. To be honest, for instance, necessarily requires thinking of honesty as an excellence worth striving for. Such valuing links motivation and insight because rational agents value things they believe to be genuinely important or worthwhile. In turn, valuing something creates motivation to promote it. Dispositionally trustworthy professionals, therefore, strive to continually develop their trustworthiness. Because conflicts of interests pose a threat to one's trustworthiness, those who are virtuous will be motivated ipso facto to avoid such conditions.

Some professionals argue that, because they are virtuous, it is inappropriate to define a conflict of interest as an action situation in which a *reasonable observer* would conclude that a professional of normal human psychology would be tempted to favor secondary over primary interests. As trained and virtuous experts, professionals sometimes argue they are immune from the temptations that would lead a person of normal psychology to stray.

There are good reasons to think, however, that this self-assessment of the strength of one's character virtues is unreliable and unrealistic. Studies on the unconscious bias created by secondary interests show that, given the right context, even small incentives can have important, and often *unconscious,* biasing effects on the judgment and conduct of professionals. This occurs through a variety of "cold" mechanisms[15] by which the mind seeks to dissolve cognitive dissonance by forming beliefs which make it seemingly possible to "have one's cake and eat it, too." These mechanisms are clearly seen in the variety of studies that show, for instance, that people tend to adopt beliefs about the nature of justice based on their personal interests.[16]

The biasing effect created by incentives can be both unintentional and unconscious. One survey of physicians, for instance, found that the majority believed that receiving gifts from pharmaceutical manufactures would have a biasing effect on the average physician's prescribing behavior. A majority of the same physicians reported that they believed that they *personally* would be immune from such bias. Such physicians believed that because they were dispositionally trustworthy and trained scientists, they are able to resist the reciprocity effect created by such gifts, and would detect any biasing in their thinking.

In light of the empirical literature both about bias and the poor reflexivity of biased agents, the view that one is uniquely immune from these mechanisms is wishful thinking and dangerous hubris. The unconscious nature of incentivized bias is such that a professional may truly believe he or she is acting appropriately when such a view is actually the result of bias. Recall that the VIGOR safety committee adopted a "naproxen as aspirin effect" hypothesis even in the absence of scientific evidence. Such "wishful thinking" is a classic mechanism of unconscious, incentivized bias.[17]

Some professionals, because they are highly educated experts who are committed to dispositional trustworthiness, *overestimate* their power of impartiality in the face of powerful incentives. For this reason, trustworthy professionals will cultivate the virtue of *humility*, lest their pride in their intellectual and moral capabilities leads them to underestimate the power of incentives in shaping their conduct. Professionals who are appropriately humble will actively avoid conflicts of interest.

Effective Trustworthiness and Conflict of Interest

Despite the effect of conflicts of interest on motivation, it is still the case that professionals often, and perhaps routinely, serve their primary interests in spite of the temptations caused by misaligned secondary interests. This might lead one to conclude that many conflicts of interest are merely "appearances" of conflict—that is, "red flags" that call for increased vigilance. From this perspective, there is nothing unethical about practicing with a conflict of interest, provided that one does not allow it to undermine one's independence of judgment.

Such a view is suspect because of the nature of unconscious bias (discussed earlier), and because even in the absence of direct influence, when professionals practice with a conflict of interest, they violate their obligation to be *effectively* trustworthy. Professionals have an obligation to invite and develop the trust of those they intend to serve. Such trust is essential to the success of professional practice and makes good on the "social bargain" between the public and the professions by which the public extends important privileges to the profession and in return receives, or should receive, reliable and trustworthy professional service. Developing trust with clients and patients also respects their personhood by recognizing them as a "Thou" whose vulnerabilities deserve responsible care.

Because trust is essential to reliable professional service, professionals have an obligation to conduct themselves in a manner conducive to the development of client and public trust. This requires that professionals be trustworthy *and* effectively communicate that trustworthiness to the public and (would be) clients. A professional is effectively trustworthy when he or she is able to successfully communicate or signal his or her possession of trust warranting properties such as relevant character virtues or encapsulated interests. Because bad character *and* poor information are enemies of trust, effective trustworthiness is an essential element in the development of client and public trust. Without effective signaling of one's trust-warranting properties, clients and the public have no way to infer that the professional is trustworthy in relatively anonymous conditions. Effective trustworthiness is achieved by professionals through (1) the development of a robust reputation for trustworthiness on the part of the professional social role, (2) the effective impression management by individual professionals, and (3) conduct that honors client and public trust. Conflicts of interest diminish the effective trustworthiness of professionals in a variety of ways.

1. Reputation:

Professional communities go to great lengths to develop robust ethical reputations for professional social types. Codes of ethics, oaths, ethics opinions, mission statements, and even advertising are communications used to bolster the reputation of professionals as trustworthy individuals who take seriously their obligation to honor the trust they solicit from clients and the public at large. When professional associations—which are key representatives of the professional community—tolerate conflicts of interest within professional practice, the reputation of the professional-role is damaged in a variety of ways. Tolerating conflicts of interest introduces legitimate doubt about the community's commitment to trustworthiness, and casts a shadow on the various efforts by the community to build up the professional reputation. Perhaps the greatest threat to the professional reputation is the suspicion that the various ethical commitments articulated by the professional community are but *window dressing*. The toleration of conflicts of interest lends credibility to such concerns.

These concerns are made all the more credible by the well-publicized cases in which conflicts of interest appear to have played a key role in professional misconduct. In Vioxx, financial incentives appear to have played a key role in the delayed recognition of the drug's dangers. In the Challenger explosion, political and financial concerns led NASA and Morton Thiokol managers to ignore engineers who believed that the launch conditions were unsafe.[18] In the subprime mortgage crisis, rating agencies were paid by the very companies whose products they were evaluating, which created powerful incentives to provide favorable ratings in order to retain and attract more business.[19] In the Enron collapse, the accounting firm Arthur Anderson was both Enron's auditor *and* consultant. In fact, Anderson made more money ($27 million) as an Enron consultant than it did as its auditor ($25 million).[20] This blurred relationship created strong incentives for Anderson to adopt lax standards when auditing Enron.

These disasters make clear to the public the real, and not merely apparent, threat that conflicts of interest create for those who are vulnerable to professional misconduct. When professional communities tolerate such conflicts, they send a powerful message to the public that despite all the rhetoric, the professional community is not particularly concerned about the trustworthiness of its members—especially when profit, power, and prestige are at stake.

2. Interpersonal Trust:

Damage to the professional reputation makes it all the more difficult for professionals to develop interpersonal trust with clients and patients. At the extreme, those with impoverished trust of professionals simply do not use them—they avoid doctors, refuse to have their children vaccinated, stuff money in mattresses, and do their own accounting. Even when clients do seek out professional assistance, the professional's task of impression management is considerably more difficult if the professional reputation has been damaged. Clients and patients may become too suspicious to consider that the impression management of the profession is in any way sincere.

This situation is exacerbated when the individual professional practices with a conflict of interest. Practicing with such conflicts creates an action context in which the signal management of the professional is likely to appear cynical and empty, with the result of preventing the formation of the robust trust necessary for effective professional practice. Even if the professional's character virtues are strong enough to overcome the temptations created by the conflict, such reliability is mere "krypta" that cannot be readily observed by clients and patients relying on relatively anonymous professionals. While the professional may be trustworthy from a god's eye perspective, he or she will not be perceived as such by the human-eye perspective of the client or patient. Because trustworthiness is only effective when it is perceived, appearances matter a great deal.

It is for this reason that potential conflicts of interest are best evaluated not from the standpoint of the individual professional, but from the perspective of the reasonable trust-evaluator who will be vulnerable to the professional's discretion and thus reliant on his or her good will and integrity. Epistemically, given the unconscious nature of incentivized bias, there are good reasons not to privilege the professional's perspective on his or her own motivations. Ethically, the reasonable trust-evaluator (e.g., client/patient) perspective is appropriate because professionals have an obligation to be effectively trustworthy—that is, to present them in a manner by which trust-evaluators can infer the professional's possession of trust warranting properties. When professionals practice in contexts in which their secondary interests would pose a serious temptation to a professional of normal psychology, they signal, perhaps unintentionally, to clients and the public that they are not trustworthy.

For these reasons, it is misleading to speak of a mere "appearance" of a conflict of interest. The perceptions created by such conflict-situations are toxic to the trust that professionals should develop in their clients, patients, and general public. Appearances matter a great deal, so much so that conflicts of interest are best evaluated from the perspective of the reasonable observer. Understood this way, many so called "apparent" conflicts of interest are true conflicts of interest.

Of course, such conflicts are only corrosive to trust if those that depend on professionals are aware of them. It is tempting, therefore, to conceal them. However tempting, this is morally unacceptable for a variety of reasons. Because knowledge of conflicts of interest can have a material effect on a trust-evaluator's decision to extend trust, concealment of them constitutes a form of *deception* that violates the basic right to autonomous decision making. Moreover, trust formed through such deception violates the widely accepted view that warranted trust must satisfy "publicity" conditions by which invitations to trust should be extended via a transparent presentation of the trustee's trust-warranting properties.[21] Trust based on deception or ignorance manipulates the trustor, treating him or her as a mere means to an end.

MANAGING CONFLICTS OF INTEREST

Because professionals have an obligation to be instrumentally, dispositionally, and effectively trustworthy, and because conflicts of interest are toxic to that trustworthiness, such conflicts are to be avoided when possible and robustly managed when unavoidable. Conflicts are *avoidable* when they are unnecessary in the performance of one's professional practice within the typical systems in which professionals work. In the Vioxx case, for instance, Dr. Weinblatt's ownership of Merck stock and his agreement to serve as a paid consultant for Merck created a conflict of interest that reduced his trustworthiness. It was also unnecessary given his role as a physician.

Avoidable conflicts of interest are therefore best managed by avoidance and divestment. When the professional can foresee the conflict, he or she has an obligation to avoid it. If an avoidable conflict emerges unexpectedly, the professional should move to divest him or herself of the relevant secondary interests or, if ethical, end the fiduciary relationship with the client or patient. When they fail to do so, professionals voluntarily choose to practice in a situation that undermines their instrumental, dispositional, and effective trustworthiness. In such cases, they are *blameworthy* for choosing to do so.

Disclosure, which is often viewed as a panacea of such conflicts, is generally insufficient for a number of reasons. Most importantly, those disclosing and "managing" the conflict are often the very same persons practicing with the conflict. This arrangement does not sufficiently protect clients, patients, and the general public from the powerful incentives to prioritize secondary interests over one's professional responsibilities. For example, in the subprime mortgage collapse, the conflicts of interest created by rating agencies being paid by the very companies whose products they were rating was well disclosed. Nonetheless, the U.S. Senate Subcommittee report on the sub-prime mortgage crises concluded:

> The credit rating agencies assured Congress and the investing public that they could "manage" these conflicts, but the evidence indicates that the drive for market share and increasing revenues, ratings shopping, and investment bank pressures have undermined the ratings process and the quality of the ratings themselves. Multiple former Moody's and S&P employees told the Subcommittee that, in the years leading up to the financial crisis, gaining market share, increasing revenues, and pleasing investment bankers bringing business to the firm assumed a higher priority than issuing accurate RMBS and CDO credit ratings. [22]

Disclosing an avoidable conflict of interest also fails to address the underlying and negative affect that such conflicts have on effective trustworthiness. While clients and the public will certainly appreciate the professional's demonstration of honesty, a reasonable client would still likely be suspicious of the professional's trustworthiness given the conflict's avoidability. Clients and patients will be more likely to adopt hedging strategies that make professional service significantly less effective. Moreover, if the professional community permits avoidable conflicts, a client or patient might acquiesce to, rather than endorse, the professional's conflict because they believe that such conflicts will be widespread among professionals of this type. This inference, in turn, leads to hedging practices and damages the professional reputation generally as community tolerance of avoidable conflicts signals a lack of concern for professional trustworthiness. In such cases, trust-evaluators such as clients, patients, and the public are likely to conclude that the variety of assurances made by the professional community regarding the virtues of those who occupy the professional role are but a cynical facade. Professionals, as individuals and as members of professional communities, therefore have good reasons to demand general standards of conduct that prohibit practicing in the context of avoidable conflicts of interest.

Finally, disclosure is insufficient because, in practice, it often provides insufficient opportunity for trust-evaluators to assesses their degree of willingness to trust the conflicted professional. Dr. Weinblatt, the chairperson of the VIGOR safety committee did, in fact, disclose his ownership of Merck stock. However, the VIGOR study participants never knew of this conflict, and so were never able to assess their willingness to trust his oversight of the study. When disclosures are not readily available to trust-evaluators, and they often are not, the effect is the same as deception, with trust-evaluators forming trust based on an inaccurate understanding of the professional's trustworthiness.

While practicing with an avoidable conflict of interest is morally blameworthy, not all conflicts are avoidable. Consider a software engineer who recommends a data security system that he or she helped invent and license. If the engineer genuinely believes that the system best serves the client, then beneficence requires that he or she recommend it. At the same time, if the sale of the system entails significant profit for the engineer, the engineer has a conflict of interest. Or consider the more endemic conflicts created by managed health care systems. In such systems physicians are expected to serve two masters—the patient and their employer. Physicians in such systems are under pressure to generate revenue, which creates a general temptation to recommend unnecessary treatments for patients.

Professionals have an obligation to avoid conflicts of interest. However, it is widely recognized that "ought implies can," and, as such, conflicts that are reasonably unavoidable are not blameworthy. Conflicts such as the software engineers are unavoidable insofar as the engineer has a duty to recommend the products that best promote the client's interest. Requiring that the engineer refrain from recommending his or her own system does not promote the client's interest and, in essence, punishes the engineer for developing new products. The case of physicians in managed care is perhaps logically avoidable, but is not reasonably so. One could, for instance, require that physicians refuse to work in for-profit managed care systems. This would be excessive, however, as many good physicians would simply not find work if they could not work in managed, for-profit institutions—and the public would ultimately suffer. As long as there are for-profit health-care markets, such as in the United States, it is unreasonable to demand that physicians avoid all such conflicts.

Reasonably unavoidable conflicts of interest are not inherently blameworthy. They are nonetheless damaging to the trustworthiness of the professional (and the profession) and call for effective and responsible management. For instance, patients who cite lower levels of trust in physicians often point to the systemic conflicts of interest created by for-profit managed care institutions. While practicing with such a conflict is not blameworthy, professionals still have an obligation, rooted in their obligation to be effectively trustworthy, to respond to such conflicts in a responsible manner. The obligation to promote trustworthiness also requires a concerted response by the professional community to mitigate their trust-corroding effect.

At the individual level, professionals should disclose unavoidable conflicts in a timely and reasonably informed manner that gives clients and patients a genuine opportunity to assess the trustworthiness of the professional. Timeliness is important because the longer disclosure is delayed, the more costly it is for clients and patients to seek out a new professional. Conflicts also need to be managed in a way that limits, as much as possible, the effects of the conflict on the effective trustworthiness of the professional. For instance, consider an orthopedic surgeon who has developed and patented a joint replacement device. The surgeon might genuinely believe the device to be the most appropriate for a particular patient, but given the profitability of the device for the surgeon, a conflict of interest is certainly present. The surgeon can manage this conflict by disclosing in timely manner the conflict and making readily available a "second opinion" to the patient. They could also divest themselves of profit they would earn from the use of their device on this particular patient. Additionally, by participating in a "joint registry" which would track the outcomes of patients receiving the relevant type of joint replacement device, the surgeon could provide objective data to patients assuring them that the recommendation is evidence-based rather than interest based.

Unavoidable conflicts can also be mitigated by institutional responses, particularly in the use of institutional constraints that counteract the effect of the conflict. For instance, the creation and maintenance of joint registries would allow inventor-surgeons to make recommendations based on demonstrable device performance, thus reassuring patients of the independence of their judgment. Or, in managed health-care settings, the incentive to "process" as many patients as possible can be counteracted through the use of patient satisfaction surveys that assess the time the physician spends with patients. Such surveys can then be used as part of the physician's compensation package. If done properly, institutional constraints can counteract the conflict such that it no longer creates a serious temptation for the physician to promote secondary interests at the expense of the patient, or can provide reassurances of the professional's independence of judgment.

In some cases, the professional community itself should advocate for changes in social systems to reduce systemic conflicts. An underlying problem in the Vioxx case, for instance, is the prominent role played by pharmaceutical manufacturers in the safety testing of their own products. This creates strong incentives, as it did with Merck and Vioxx, to manipulate clinical trials in ways favorable to the corporate bottom line. This led Merck to create conflicts of interest on the part of professionals, such as Dr. Weinblatt, that incentivized judgments favorable to the company. The medical community has good reasons to call for changes to the regulatory system so that physicians and researchers are not placed in such systemic conflicts of interest.

PROFESSIONAL ASSOCIATIONS AND ORGANIZATIONAL CONFLICT OF INTEREST

Conflicts of interest, such as those in the Vioxx case, involve situations in which professionals practice in arrangements in which a reasonable observer would conclude that a professional of normal psychology would be tempted to promote secondary interests at the expense of professional responsibilities.

However, conflicts can also be more systemic in situations in which professional *organizations* are incentivized to promote secondary interests over professional responsibilities. Because of the important role they play in developing standards of training, credentialing, and ethical conduct, professional associations are taken to be the de facto representatives of the profession, both by the public and by professional community members themselves. Professional associations have good reasons, therefore, to invite and develop trust from those they serve.

The primary interests of professional associations are quite different from those of trade associations. Consider the key goals articulated in the mission statement of the National Society of Professional Engineers: "Through education, licensure, advocacy, leadership training, multidisciplinary networking, and outreach, NSPE enhances the image of its members and their ability to ethically and professionally practice engineering."[23] The mission statement of the American Bar Association states as its primary goal: "To serve equally our members, our profession and the public by defending liberty and delivering justice as the national representative of the legal profession."[24] And the American Medical Association states as its key vision: "[i]mproving the health of the nation is at the core of the AMA's work to enhance the delivery of care and enable physicians and health teams to partner with patients to achieve better health for all."[25]

These sentiments are more than "motherhood" statements. They are reflected and concretized in a variety of institutional mechanisms by which professional associations are key players in creating trustworthy professionals, both as individuals and as members of flourishing ethical communities. It is professional associations that create and promulgate codes of ethics, create standards of training and technical competence, create proficiency exams used by licensing boards, sponsor journals and conferences that promote the technical and ethical discourses of the profession, and recommend discipline for members engaging in unethical conduct. Professional associations also play a key role in the development and maintenance of the reputation of the professional social type, a reputation necessary for the anonymous trust formed by those who depend on professionals.

For these reasons, members of professional associations—especially the leaders of these associations—have an obligation to invite, develop, and honor the trust they secure from the public and from members of the profession. While professional associations rightly seek to advance the financial interests of their members, it must be remembered that the *primary* interest of their members is the achievement of the internal goods of the profession—goods such as health, safety, justice, and financial security. The primary interests of professional associations include, as their mission statements indicate, the promotion of these goods. Because the promotion of these goods requires the trust of clients, patients, students and the general public, professional associations have an obligation to promote effective trustworthiness in the profession, in part by being effectively trustworthy themselves.

Because of their obligation to be effectively trustworthy, when professional associations operate with an avoidable conflict of interest, they are morally blameworthy. A professional association has a conflict of interest when it operates with arrangements that a reasonable observer would conclude a significant temptation exists for the organization to favor secondary interests (e.g., money and prestige) at the expense of its professional responsibilities. These conflicts can be based on the interests of individual members (particularly leadership) or the decision-making procedure or culture of the association itself.

An association has a conflict of interest when members of its leadership have conflicts by which their secondary interests create significant temptations to neglect their duties as leaders of professional associations. For instance, if the leadership of a medical association is financially invested in, or financially dependent on, a particular medical device manufacturer, there will be strong temptations to make decisions that benefit that manufacturer at the expense of the primary mission of the association. This conflict might result in the way that the association's conference program is selected. If the association tolerates (and perhaps encourages) a program selection committee that is itself highly invested in, or dependent on, the manufacturer, then there will be strong temptations for the conference program to reflect papers favorable to that manufacturer. Given the nature of unconscious bias discussed earlier, the program selection committee members themselves could not be certain they created a program based on independent judgment. Meanwhile, rank and file members see the conflicted nature of the association, casting its work under a cloud of suspicion.

For this reason, some commentators have argued that the leadership of a professional association, at least during their leadership tenure, should have *no* avoidable conflicts of interest.[26] With leadership comes responsibility, and this may require those interested in leading professional associations to divest financial interests that would conflict with the responsibilities of the association. For far too long, associations have allowed deeply conflicted professionals to serve as leaders of professional organizations with the idea that disclosure of such conflict is ethically sufficient. For the reasons already outlined, disclosure is not a sufficient strategy for dealing with avoidable conflicts of interest. A professional association that tolerates such conflicts jeopardizes its moral integrity and sends a strong signal to the public, and to members of the professional community, that it does not take its effective trustworthiness seriously.

Conflicted leadership is not the only form of organizational conflict of interest. The secondary interests of the association qua association can also create such conflicts. This occurs, for instance, when professional associations enter contractual arrangements with industry in ways that threaten the integrity of the association's decision-making process, regardless of its leadership. This can be seen in the controversial relationship between the American Academy of Family Physicians and Coca-Cola.

Organizational Conflict of Interest: Have a Coke, $3.5 Million, and a Smile

On October 6, 2009 the American Academy of Family Physicians announced a corporate partnership with Coca-Cola:

> The Consumer Alliance is a program that allows corporate partners like The Coca-Cola Company to work with the AAFP to educate consumers about the role their products can play in a healthy, active lifestyle. As part of this partnership, The Coca-Cola Company is providing a grant to the AAFP to develop consumer education content on beverages and sweeteners for FamilyDoctor.org, an award-winning consumer health and wellness resource . . .
>
> While the AAFP does not endorse any specific brand, product or service, the AAFP Consumer Alliance will collaborate with companies that share the common goal of informing consumers, as well as medical professionals, about new advances in product science and best practices for good health.[27]

Such an alliance was puzzling for a number of reasons. Most experts in the field point to soft drink consumption as a major contributor to obesity, especially in young people. Having a soft drink company help "educate" consumers about the "best practices for good health" seems akin to, as one critic put it, "a deal with Phillip Morris to educate people about smoking, a partnership with Seagram's to discourage alcohol misuse, and an alliance with Colt's Manufacturing to combat gun violence."[28]

Making the alliance even more puzzling (at least from the perspective of a respected medical association) was the soft drink industry's marketing campaign advancing the dubious claim that obesity problems in American are caused primarily by lack of exercise, not overconsumption. This campaign was developed in response to a variety of proposals to tax, or even ban, soft-drink products. In an apparently coordinated marketing effort, the AAFP partnership announcement was followed *the very next day* by an editorial by Muhtar Kent, CEO of Coca-Cola in the *Wall Street Journal* entitled, "Coke Didn't Make America Fat: Americans Need More Exercise, Not Another Tax." Kent concluded, "[b]usiness and government should come together to help encourage greater physical activity and sensible eating and drinking, while allowing Americans to enjoy the simple pleasure of a Coca-Cola."[29]

In other ways, the partnership between the AAFP and Coca-Cola was not puzzling at all. The AAFP was looking for ways to diversify its revenue stream, especially away from pharmaceutical companies, and saw such corporate partnerships as means to do so. For its part, Coca-Cola had in interest in steering the discourse on obesity and gained, or thought it would gain, credibility in the debate by partnering with a variety of health organizations. The company's support of the AAFP was significant—between October 2009 and June 2015 it provided the AAFP with more than $3.5 million. [30]

In this particular case the AAFP chose to create what Howard Brody calls an "organizational conflict of interest." [31] As a medical professional organization committed to, as expressed in its own vision statement, "a leadership role in advancing the health of the public," [32] the primary interests of the AAFP is the promotion of public health. It invites the trust of the public and members of the profession in light of this stated goal. But this invitation to trust is irrational and manipulative if it is not coupled with an organizational commitment to be, and to effectively communicate, its trustworthiness.

Given Coca-Cola's significant support, a reasonable observer would conclude that the organization would be "tempted" to make a variety of decisions favorable to Coca-Cola and its "exercise centric" message, at the expense of public health. Could the organization now be trusted to create objective and independent educational material when Coca-Cola lavishly funded those materials? Numerous observers concluded it could not. Indeed, media outlets described the alliance as a "sell out" [33] and a number of AAFP members resigned in protest of the move. Dr. William Walker, Director of the Contra Costa, CA Department of Health Services wrote when resigning from his twenty-five-year membership:

> I am appalled and ashamed of this partnership between Coca-Cola and the American Academy of Family Physicians. How can any organization that claims to promote public health join forces with a company that promotes products that put our children at risk for obesity, heart disease and early death? [34]

Another AAFP member commented "[m]y Academy's decision to partner with Coca-Cola sends exactly the wrong message to my patients at exactly the wrong time." [35]

Such conflicts of interest are "organizational" in that once such an arrangement has been created, there is an incentive for members of the organization to sacrifice the organization's responsibilities in order to promote the relevant secondary interest. Changing leadership will not resolve such conflicts because the incentives are not specific to any particular leader, but to the arrangements to which the organization itself has been committed. The conflicting incentive becomes a part of the decision-making process of the organization itself.

Linda Heim, president of the AAFP, contented that one could not criticize the deal with Coca-Cola until there was evidence that the arrangement had undermined the objectivity of the educational materials produced by the AAFP. In her view, any apparent conflict created by the corporate partnership was merely a "red flag" calling for vigilance. Any biasing effect could be ethically managed with disclosure and transparency.[36] Howard Brody countered that the "wait and see" attitude of the AAFP misses the point of professional ethics, which is to be provide *ex ante* evaluation of conduct in order to *prevent* breaches of trust. A judge who own $100,000 dollars of stock in a company that is a litigant in a trial over which he or she presides can hardly offer as a defense, "my conflict is not unethical until you see how I decide the case."[37]

Conflicts of interest undermine the effective trustworthiness of individuals and organizations. Even in the absence of malfeasance, inviting and maintaining avoidable conflicts of interest signals to the professional community and to the public that the association is willing to risk its integrity to promote its financial interests. Were it a for-profit business, such risk would be understandable, but as a medical association that has as a key objective assuming "a leadership role in advancing the health of the public,"[38] such a risk is unacceptable. Professional associations are leaders of professional communities and offer themselves as valuable participants in public discourse. To make good on their commitments, they must be effectively trustworthy. Voluntarily entering, indeed promoting, conflicts of interest weakens the association's claim that it is worthy of public, client/patient, and member trust.

Conflict of Interest and Discourse Colonization

Conflicts of interest on the part of professional associations are especially dangerous given the central role such associations play in the ongoing expert and ethical discourses of the profession. Professional associations sponsor journals, major conferences, newsletters, informational websites, and continuing education seminars. They often play an important role in shaping regulations and legislation in their area of professional expertise. When professional associations become conflicted, there is a very real possibility that private interests will "colonize" professional discourse.

Discourse colonization occurs when a justificatory discourse, which should be transparent and oriented toward consensus based on rational persuasion, becomes dominated instead by the steering mechanisms of money and power.[39] When conflicted, professional organizations have a strong incentive to tolerate or promote similar conflicts on the part of journal editors, peer reviewers, conference organizers, and designers of educational material.

The effort by the soft drink industry to colonize the discourse on obesity is a good example of these dangers. In the face of the best evidence, the soft drink company launched an aggressive campaign to reshape the scientific discourse on obesity from diet-centric to exercise-centric. It not only provided large "educational" grants to the AAFP ($3.5 million), but also to the American College of Cardiology ($3.1 million), The American Academy of Pediatrics (nearly $3 million), The American Cancer Society ($2 million), and the Academy of Nutrition and Dietetics ($1.7 million).[40] It additionally funded nonprofit organizations and researchers who supported its exercise-centric vision of obesity. In all of these cases, the purpose of these funds was to gain leverage with key medical institutions in order for them to promote, or at least not actively resist, its exercise-centric marketing campaign. Indeed, critics contended that the final educational materials produced for the AAFP did, in fact, underemphasize the role of sugary soft drinks in obesity.[41]

At the very least, the AAFP lent legitimacy to Coca-Cola's campaign by providing links on its educational website to Coca-Cola's own "educational" site, where the exercise-centric message was the singular theme. One such ironic instance occurred on the AAFP's page on diabetes which encouraged a sound diet while providing a prominent link to Coca-Cola's "exercise first" website, and identifying Coca-Cola as a "partial underwriter" of the page.[42]

The partnerships with medical professional associations also provided credibility to Coca-Cola's suspect claim that it was genuinely concerned about fighting obesity. Muhtar Kent, in his *Wall Street Journal* editorial, (again published the day after the announcement of its partnership with the AAFP) argued that the company was committed to working with "health organizations" in its effort to fight obesity.[43] Partnering with medical associations such as the AAFP worked hand-in-hand with the company's direct funding of researchers and/or their institutions that supported its exercise-centric message. Researchers funded by the soft drink industry were much more likely to reach conclusions favorable to their sponsors than independent researchers. Perhaps the most insidious of these efforts occurred in the creation of the Global Energy Balance Network, which claimed to be an independent group of researchers advocating for obesity reduction. The group was eventually forced to acknowledge that it was largely funded by Coca-Cola, and a damning series of disclosed emails showed the organization's leadership working closely with Coca-Cola executives in orienting the organization's activities.[44]

While the soft drink industry was colonizing the medical discourse and the public policy debate on obesity, key medical associations such as the AAFP, which should have been leading the charge against such efforts, did little. Indeed, they assisted the effort by providing credibility to Coca-Cola's efforts to partner with health organizations. To the degree that their educational sites reflected dampened criticisms of soft drink consumption they were also complicit in this colonization. But even if they did not, these associations offered Coca-Cola credibility as a partner in its "fight" against obesity, and as such became, perhaps unwittingly, partners in Coca-Cola's efforts to colonize the discourse on obesity.

Coca-Cola's efforts, and those of the soft drink industry generally, were criticized and ultimately exposed, though sadly not by key medical associations, but instead by individual physicians, researchers, bioethicists, and news media outlets. By 2015 the colonizing effort had been sufficiently exposed to damage the Coca-Cola brand. In an apologetic editorial in the *Wall Street Journal*, Muhtar Kent acknowledged that Coca-Cola's efforts "have served only to create more confusion and mistrust."[45] In June 2015 the AAFP announced that it and Coca-Cola had mutually agreed to end their partnership.

CONCLUSION

Professionals have good reasons, including a moral obligation, to invite, develop and honor the trust of those that depend on them. Conflicts of interest occur when a professional practices in arrangements that a reasonable onlooker would conclude that a person of normal psychology would be tempted to favor secondary interests (typically money and prestige) at the expense of their professional responsibilities. Choosing to practice in an avoidable conflict of interest is blameworthy, even in the absence of direct malfeasance, because it is inconsistent with the professional obligation to be effectively trustworthy. Professional associations have a similar obligation to avoid conflicts of interest and responsibly manage those that are unavoidable. Given their important role in the work of the profession as an ethical community, it is especially important the professional associations transcend the work of trade associations—which often take as their primary interest the financial well-being of their members—and take seriously their obligation to be effectively trustworthy organizations by scrupulously avoiding conflicts of interest when possible, while rigorously disclosing and management conflicts that are unavoidable.

NOTES

1. Snigda Prakash, "Conflicted Safety Panel Let Vioxx Study Continue," *National Public Radio*, June 8, 2006. http://www.npr.org/templates/story/story.php?storyId=5462419
2. Holly Presley, "Vioxx and the Merck Team Effort," *The Kenan Institute for Ethics at Duke University* (2009): 8. https://web.duke.edu/kenanethics/CaseStudies/Vioxx.pdf.
3. Snigda Prakash and Vikki Valentine, "Timeline: The Rise and Fall of Vioxx," *National Public Radio*, November 10, 2007, http://www.npr.org/templates/story/story.php?story/Id=5470430
4. Prakash and Valentine, "Timeline: The Rise and Fall of Vioxx."
5. Presley, "Vioxx and the Merck Team Effort," 7.
6. Melody Petersen, "Doubts are Raised About the Safety of 2 Popular Arthritis Drugs," *New York Times*, May 22, 2001.
7. David J Graham, David Campen, Rita Hui, Michele Spence, Craig Cheetham, Gerald Levy, Stanford Shoor, Wayne Ray, "Risk of Acute Myocardial Infarction and Sudden Cardiac

Death in Patients Treated with Cyclo-oxygenase 2 Selective and Non-Selective Non-Steroidal Anti-Inflammatory Drugs: Nested Case Control Study," *The Lancet* 365, no. 9458 (2005): 480.

8. Prakash and Valentine, "Timeline: The Rise and Fall of Vioxx."

9. Prakash, "Conflicted Safety Panel Let Vioxx Study Continue."

10. Institute of Medicine, "Conflict of Interest and Development of Clinical Practice Guidelines," in *Conflict of Interest in Medical Research, Education, and Practice.* (Washington, DC: The National Academies Press; 2009): 189–215.

11. Howard Brody, "Clarifying Conflict of Interest," *American Journal of Bioethics* 11, no.1 (2011): 24. See also, Edmund Erde, "Conflicts of Interest in Medicine: A Philosophical and Ethical Morphology," in *Conflicts of Interest in Clinical Practice and Research,* ed. Roy Speece, David Shim and Allen Buchanan (New York: Oxford University Press, 1996), 12–41.

12. Prakash, "Conflicted Safety Panel Let Vioxx Study Continue."

13. Neil Luebke, "Conflict of Interest as a Moral Category," *Business & Professional Ethics Journal* 6 (1987): 66–81.

14. Aristotle, *Nicomachean Ethics,* trans. William Irwin (Indianapolis: Hackett Publishing Company, 1999), 103.

15. Jon Elster, *Sour Grapes* (Cambridge, MA: Cambridge University Press, 1983), 26.

16. Jason Dana and George Lowenstein, "A Social Science Perspective on Gifts to Physicians from Industry," *Journal of the American Medical Association* 290, no. 2 (2003). Mahzarin Banaji and Anthony Greenwald, *Blindspot: Hidden Biases of Good People* (New York: Delacorte Press, 2013).

17. Jon Elster, *Sour Grapes*, 148–67.

18. Davis, "Thinking Like an Engineer," 150–51.

19. Senate Subcommittee on Permanent Investigations, *Wall Street and the Financial Crises: An Anatomy of a Financial Collapse,* U.S. Senate (2011): 272–73. http://www.hsgac .senate.gov//imo/media/doc/Financial_Crisis/FinancialCrisisReport.pdf?attempt=2

20. Thaddeus Herrick and Alexie Barrionuevo, "Were Enron, Anderson Too Close to Allow Auditor to Do Its Job," *Wall Street Journal,* January 21, 2002.

21. Annette Baier, "Trust and Antitrust," *Ethics* 96, no. 2 (1986): 255.

22. Senate Subcommittee on Permanent Investigations, *Wall Street and the Financial Crisis,* 273.

23. "NSPE Strategic Plan," National Society of Professional Engineers, accessed June 8, 2016, http://www.nspe.org/membership/nspe-who-we-are-what-we-do/nspe-strategic-plan# sthash.3UZHRMw8.dpuf

24. "Mission and Goals," American Bar Association, accessed June 8, 2016, http:// www.americanbar.org/about_the_aba/aba-mission-goals.html

25. "Strategic Focus," American Medical Association, accessed June 10, 2016, http:// www.ama-assn.org/ama/pub/about-ama/strategic-focus.page?

26. David Rothman, et. al. "Professional Medical Associations and Their Relation to Industry," *Journal of the American Medical Association* 301, no. 13 (2009): 1367–72.

27. "The American Academy of Family Physicians Launches Consumer Alliance with First Partner: The Coca-Cola Company," American Academy of Family Physicians, accessed May 5, 2016, http://www.aafp.org/media-center/releases-statements/all/2009/consumeralliance-co-cacola.html

28. Jeff Sussman, "Do Things Really Go Better with Coke," *Journal of Family Practice* 58, no. 12 (2009): 630.

29. Muhtar Kent, "Coke Didn't Make America Fat," *Wall Street Journal*, October 7, 2009.

30. Anahad O'Connor, "Coke Spends Lavishly on Pediatricians and Dieticians," *New York Times,* September 28, 2015.

31. Howard Brody, "Medical Organizations and Commercial Conflicts of Interest: Ethical Issues," *Annals of Family Medicine* 8 (2010): 354–58.

32. "Vision," American Academy of Family Physicians, accessed June 1, 2016, http:// www.aafp.org/about/the-aafp/vision.html

33. Marion Nestle, "Why Did Doctors Sell Out to Coke," *The Atlantic,* October 11, 2009, http://www.theatlantic.com/health/archive/2009/10/why-did-doctors-sell-out-to-coke/28228/

34. "Dr. Walker Resigns Membership in American Academy of Family Physicians to Protest Its Partnership with Coca-Cola," Contra Costa Health Services, accessed March 10, 2016, http://cchealth.org/healthservices/aafp_protest.php

35. John Spangler, "Family Medicine's Sweet Tooth—for Money," *ABC News*, November 16, 2009, http://abcnews.go.com/Health/Wellness/coke-partnership-aafp-angers-doctors/story?id=9079376

36. Linda Heim, "Identifying and Addressing Potential Conflicts of Interest: A Professional Medical Organization's Code of Ethics," *Annals of Family Medicine* 8, no. 4 (2010): 359–61.

37. Brody, "Professional Medical Organizations and Commercial Conflicts of Interest: Ethical Issues," 356.

38. "Vision," American Academy of Family Physicians.

39. Jürgen Habermas, *The Theory of Communicative Action Vol. 2*, trans. Thomas McCarthy (Boston: Beacon Press, 1987).

40. Anahad O'Connor, "Coke Discloses Millions in Grants for Health Research and Community Programs," *New York Times,* September 22, 2015.

41. Yoni Freedhof, "Proof the AAFP Sold Out to Coca-Cola?" *Weighty Matters* (blog), January 5, 2010, http://www.weightymatters.ca/2010/01/proof-aafp-sold-out-to-coca-cola.html.

42. Richard Bruno and Kevin Burns, "The Not-So-Sweet-Relief: How the Soda Industry Is Influencing Medical Associations," *The Equation* (blog), Union of Concerned Scientists, October 15, 2014, http://blog.ucsusa.org/science-blogger/the-not-so-sweet-relief-how-the-soda-industry-is-influencing-medical-organizations-683

43. Kent, "Coke Didn't Make America Fat."

44. Anihad O'Connor, "Research Group Funded by Coca-Cola to Disband," *New York Times,* December 1, 2015.

45. Muhtar Kent, "Coca-Cola: We'll Do Better," *Wall Street Journal,* August 19, 2015.

Chapter Seven

The Limits to Professional Trustworthiness

The essence of professional practice is an offer of effective expert assistance. Because of this, professionals have good instrumental, ethical, and moral reasons to invite, develop, and honor the trust of those who depend on them—clients, patients, peers, employers, and the general public. By inviting trust and offering assurances of their trustworthiness, professionals make an implied promise to responsibly care for the interests entrusted to them. However, there are genuine ethical limits to the scope of the invitation to trust made by professionals. This is because professionals are not simply "hired guns" to serve at the pleasure of those who depend on them. Professionals are moral agents engaged in a richly normative practice that has as its telos the achievement of valuable goods—health, safety, justice, and so on.

The professional invitation to trust, and the obligation to honor it, must be interpreted in light of the promotion of those goods and the professional community's judgment as to how those goods are responsibly achieved. Professionals must therefore approach their practice with a normative point of view that can be called "professional moral agency." The exercise of this moral agency requires professionals to transcend simple agent-principal relationships and become responsible practitioners whose practice is limited by law *and* professional obligations. As responsible practitioners, professionals restrict their service to others in ways that accord with the telos of the profession. This chapter examines two such cases: refusal of service and whistle-blowing.

AGAINST THE AGENCY MODEL OF PROFESSIONALISM

An important reason why clients fail to respect professional moral agency is the mistaken belief that professionals are but mere agents with the sole duty implementing the client's will. Certainly, this is true in simple "agent-principal" relationships. In those relationships the responsibility "for analyzing the problem, considering alternatives, solutions, deciding among the alternatives and becoming educated" lies entirely with the principal (e.g., the client).[1] Consider the agent-principle relationship between a day trader and a stockbroker. The day trader does his or her own research, determines a course of action, and then places an order through the broker. In such cases, the broker's only responsibility is to carry out the trader's order within the limits of the law.

In the agency model, the professional is merely an *instrument* that carries out the will of the principal. Indeed, various "e-trading" programs allow day traders to simply replace the broker with a computer. For this reason, when professionals are viewed as agents, there is a fundamental tendency to de-humanize them and ignore their moral autonomy. As agents, professionals are but "phantoms" who bring none of their personality to their work. The primary duty of such phantoms is to carry out the will of the principal, and if they do not do so, then pressuring, cajoling, and perhaps even threatening them to do so is appropriate. It is, after all, *their job* to carry out the client's will.

There are, however, good reasons to believe that the agency model is inappropriate for most client-professional relationships and misunderstands the service ideal of professionalism. Consider a couple seeking the advice of a financial advisor in planning for their retirement. In this case, the clients likely do not yet understand the various problems presented by planning carefully for retirement, nor the possible solutions to those problems. It is precisely this lack of knowledge that leads them to seek out the expert assistance of a financial advisor. In such cases, the responsibilities of the professional are far more extensive. Given the knowledge asymmetries at play, the professional has a responsibility to educate and deliberate *with* the clients to identify and implement the best possible actions. Far from being a mere instrument, the financial advisor is a guide, educator, and codeliberator. While the final decision must be the client's, the process of reaching that outcome is very much a jointly deliberative one. Because the clients must depend on the financial advisor's expertise, they must entrust to the professional key personal interests. For this reason, professional-client relationships transcend the simple agent-principle relationship and become *fiduciary* in character.

Understood broadly, a fiduciary relationship occurs when individual A entrusts B with discretionary power over an important interest.[2] By accepting this discretionary power, B has an obligation to responsibly promote that interest. In the day trader-broker example, there is no discretionary care entrusted to the professional, and for that reason the broker has no obligation to promote the best interests of the client. Most professional relationships are quite different—as in the financial planner case—because the professional's expert assistance entails discretionary care oriented toward the promotion of the client's best interests.

The agency model also tends to be an inappropriate model of the professional-client relationship because professionals make an implied promise to their clients, their peers, and the public at large that their conduct will be robustly ethical. Consequently, while trustworthy professionals are loyal to clients, that loyalty cannot be, and is not promised to be, absolute. When clients request services that create serious harm to the public, or are inappropriate given the telos of the professional practice, loyalty to the client must give way to other professional obligations. For this reason, while a distinctive feature of the professions is their service ideal to clients, the service they rightfully provide to clients is by no means unlimited, nor is it limited simply by law. Because of the fiduciary commitments that normatively and functionally structure professional practice, professional service is a *moral enterprise*[3] and as such has legitimate ethical and moral limits.

For instance, the telos of medicine is the promotion of health and the relief of suffering. Physicians make fiduciary commitments to patients, their peers, and the public that they can be trusted to satisfy this telos in a responsible manner. This commitment is the basis of trust between physicians, their patients, peers, and the public. This means that while patients have every right to expect physicians to respect patient autonomy, they should not trust physicians to perform procedures that are alien to the telos of medicine. Doctors have no obligation to provide contraindicated therapies, nor do they have a duty to acquiesce to a patient's refusal of therapeutic treatment without at least counseling the patient to do otherwise. Unlike the broker who simply places whatever legal order the day-trader determines, physicians have an obligation to help evaluate the means and ends chosen by the patient and to practice within the legitimate scope of the professional telos.

Professionals invite trust not only from their clients, but from the general public as well. For this reason they also have obligations that supersede the immediate client-professional relationship. This is most clear in the various engineering professions, which make clear in their ethics codes that the *primary* duty of the engineer is to the public. Service to the client must be consistent with public welfare. For this reason, clients should not expect a software engineer to create a records database with insufficient data security measures, even if that is what the client wants. The software engineer must also consider the harm caused to others (e.g., employees and customers) that an insecure database could cause.

Because professional service is guided by ethical commitments, the trust invited by professionals is not global, but must be understood in the context of the telos of the profession and the diverse commitments they have made to the variety of parties who have extended their trust to them. When professionals exercise their professional moral agency, they must balance these various commitments and, at times, limit their loyalty to those they serve. Two well-known cases of this occur when professionals refuse to provide inappropriate service, and in "whistleblowing" where they disclose wrongdoing on the part of the client or employer.

REFUSAL OF SERVICE

Professionals have an obligation to be loyal to clients, patients, and, to a lesser extent, employers. However, that obligation is not absolute. Take, for example, a patient who a requests treatment that has no therapeutic value, but comes with a variety of risks—perhaps a patient who clearly has the flu, but demands antibiotics. Suppose further this patient was willing to pay "out of pocket" for the medication.

Were physicians merely agents of patients, "respect for patient autonomy" might mean obedience to the patient limited only by the law. However, because medicine is a moral enterprise, a physician's duty to serve a patient is limited both by law *and* the ethico-moral commitments he or she makes as a physician. These commitments rightly limit the scope of trust physicians invite from patients, and create competing duties that limit the legitimate service a physician may provide. In such cases, physicians are well within their rights to refuse such requests for a number of reasons. Given the telos of medicine—promoting health and relieving suffering—physicians invite patients to entrust them with the promotion of their health, or the relief of their suffering. When a patient request aims at neither it falls outside the scope of the trust that physicians are obligated to invite from patients. As it falls outside the legitimate scope of trust physicians should invite from patients, it falls outside their professional role obligations.

Physicians invite patients to trust that they will promote their health, which entails the minimal duty of nonmalfeasance—"do no harm." This duty is rooted in the unique and invited vulnerability that patients assume vis-à-vis their physicians when they agree to trust them. It is also derived from the promise-like commitments that physicians make to the general public and to their peers that they will abide by strict ethical standards in their professional practice. For these reasons, physicians are not only permitted to refuse inappropriate service, they have a *duty* to decline to practice in a way that harms clients or patients with no particular benefit. For instance, a patient who abuses opioids might trust his or her physician to prescribe such medications to support his or her habit. However, a physician would be wrong to honor this trust as it falls outside the legitimate scope of medical practice and violates the commitments the physician makes to the public and his or her peers to responsibly advance the health of the patient. Physicians, both as individuals and as members of professional communities, invite trust in part by promising to "do no harm" and to promote the health of patients. When fueling a patient's opioid addiction, the physician violates those commitments and is no longer worthy of the trust of patients, peers, and the public.

Physicians also have a duty to refrain from such practices because of the harm they cause nonconsenting third parties. Futile treatments are not free; someone must pay for them. Typically such costs are borne by insurance carriers and, therefore, the pool of the insured. While the needs of insurance carriers should not trump the obligations a physician has to patients, when there are no such obligations, physicians have an obligation to avoid creating costs that serve no health-related purpose. Even in the case of a patient willing pay for his or her own medicine, inappropriate practices, such as over-prescribing antibiotics, pose a public health threat in the form of resistant forms of bacteria that reduce the therapeutic effectiveness of antibiotics. Overprescribing opioids creates addiction which itself results in a variety of negative outcomes for patients and the public. Because the public itself is vulnerable to the acts of physicians, a vulnerability invited by the medical community, physicians have an obligation to promote public health as well.

One should not take this point too far. Professionals invite client trust through assurances they will respect client autonomy. Professionals may not, therefore, deceive clients or act without their consent simply because it promotes the professional telos. Likewise, refusal of service is a serious matter that goes to the heart of the professional's offer of reliable and trustworthy expert assistance. A decision to refuse service must be carefully considered in light of the *appropriate* loyalty and autonomy owed to the client or patient. Because many professional decisions involve the assessment of risks versus benefits, and because those decisions are typically value-laden, professionals should typically deliberate with clients, but respect their autonomy. Requests that have no benefit or are clearly outside the scope of responsible professional practice should be refused.

CONSCIENTIOUS OBJECTION

Refusal of service is legitimate when the client or patient makes requests that are inappropriate given the telos of the profession, or violates the professional's other professional obligations. However, refusal of service is much more controversial, and difficult to justify, when the client or patient requests a legitimate service that is permissible within the scope of the professional's role obligations, but violates the professional's *personal* moral views.

In *conscientious objection*, professionals refuse service to clients or patients for just such reasons. For instance, physicians and nurses cite conscientious objection when refusing to participate in legitimate medical services such as abortion, euthanasia, or physician-assisted suicide (in states where such service is legal). Pharmacists have cited it when refusing to fill a prescription for emergency contraception; and social workers have cited it when refusing to perform an adoption home study because the prospective parents are a same-sex couple. Famously, Kentucky county clerk Kim Davis cited conscientious objection in refusing to grant marriage licenses to same-sex couples. In each of these cases, patients, clients, or the pubic are denied a legal and legitimate professional service because of the professional's personal moral views.

Were professionals simply agents, conscientious objection would be absolutely unacceptable because the core duty of the professional would be performance of requested (and legal) services. However, professionals are trustworthy, in part, because they are not simply agents, but fiduciaries who exercise moral agency when caring for the vulnerability of those they serve. For this reason, professional moral agency is a necessary element of the appropriately trustworthy professional.

Defenders of conscientious objection take this point further and argue that the respect accorded to professional moral agency should be extended to *personal* moral agency as well. After all, they argue, one cannot have a moral obligation to act in ways that are immoral, and the very integrity that makes professionals trustworthy means that good professionals will also feel compelled to honor the full range of their moral duties, not just those sanctioned by the professional community. Moreover, if professionals were *forced* to act against their personal moral beliefs, they would participate in the self-destruction of their own moral integrity, which can cause significant emotional and psychological trauma.[4] Requiring self-damaging action is itself morally objectionable, but is unjust in a liberal, pluralistic society based on the idea of reasonable respect for the diversity of persons. Defenders of strong versions of conscientious objection, such as Edmund Pellegrino, conclude that it is best thought of as a balance between the moral autonomy of the physician and that of the patient.[5]

Critics have objected that these arguments ignore the unique nature, indeed the entire point, of professionalism. The very essence of professional practice is the offer of reliable and trustworthy expert assistance. Because of the importance of such assistance, the professions are granted a unique status in society by which they secure cultural prestige and varying degrees of self-governance in their areas of expertise. Many professions are relatively self-governing *monopolies* of critical social services via their role in licensing and credentialing requirements. Moreover, professional communities are granted significant authority in determining the qualifications, training, standards, and discipline within professional practice.

The legal endorsement and public support of the professions entails a significant vulnerability on the part of the public. For instance, if one needs antibiotics for an ear infection, *one has no choice* but to seek out a licensed member of the medical profession. In this way, the physician and patient are not in a morally symmetrical situation. Patients are already vulnerable to medical professionals because of public policies that mandate their reliance on those professionals for a variety of social services. Patient rights have already been compromised in keeping the public's end of the bargain it makes with professionals. Patients rightly ascribe to physicians an obligation to make good on their end of bargain by reliably providing legal and professionally legitimate services.

When private conscience is used to refuse legal and professionally legitimate service, the reliability of the profession as a whole is cast in doubt. For instance, citing the need to preserve moral integrity, a racist professional could refuse service to African Americans. Or consider a physician who refuses to prescribe pain medication because he or she believed that pain is a sign of sin?[6] Such professionals would not be trustworthy, nor would professional communities that permitted such conduct.

A general right to conscientious objection among professionals could also lead to situations in which legal and legitimate services are simply not available at all to clients and patients. One might argue that the refusal of a single physician, nurse, social worker, or pharmacist does not affect the reliability of the professional as a whole, but this is mistaken. The refusal of individual practitioners can harm clients and patients by delaying access to legitimate professional services. In one infamous case, a Wisconsin pharmacist refused to fill a valid prescription for emergency contraception for a rape victim, who then became pregnant and had an abortion.[7]

Refusal of service based on conscientious objection also can create significant inconvenience, as clients and patients would have to "shop" for other professionals willing to provide the legal and legitimate service. And what if no others are willing to provide the service in the areas in which the client or patient resides? For instance, if pharmacists have a general right to conscientious objection, then the availability of legal, legitimate, and prescribed medication to a patient in a rural area could be made next to impossible.

This leads some medical ethicists to argue that accommodating strong rights to conscientious objection, while still maintaining the profession's reliability, would require the creation of regulatory bodies to ensure that adequate access to services would be available on a region-by-region basis.[8] Indeed, the use of conscientious objection to refuse service in abortion cases has in many places created a situation in which patients must travel hundreds of miles to access legal and legitimate services. A broad right to conscientious objection in medicine would lead, as Julian Savulescu puts it, "to a Pandora's box of idiosyncratic, bigoted, discriminatory medicine."[9]

Professionals secure the social trust of the public by their assurances—their promises—that they will provide reliable expert assistance. A broad right to conscientious objection in which the professional's moral autonomy is placed on par with that of the client or patient is simply not compatible with those assurances. For this reason, there simply cannot be a *general* right to professional conscientious objection rooted in the idea of moral integrity.

Defenders of conscientious objection argue that denying a general right to conscientious objection violates the idea of liberal neutrality by coercing individuals to abandon their values. However, this is not so. The professions are legally constituted and publicly supported because they are mutually beneficial social arrangements. Professionals voluntarily help themselves to the benefits of the profession, while the public receives reliable and trustworthy expert assistance. *No one is forced* to become a professional. However, if one chooses to do so, one voluntarily avails oneself of the cultural, social, and economic benefits of the position. As a matter of reciprocal justice, or "fair play," one has an obligation to reliably provide legal and professionally legitimate service. Individuals who cannot make this promise should not choose to become professionals.

Limited Conscientious Objection

While a strong right to conscientious objection cannot be justified by appeal to moral integrity and liberal neutrality, it may be possible to justify a weaker version of it in the mutual respect for personhood between professional and client. The fiduciary professional relationship requires a "second-person," I-Thou orientation from the professional to the client. Viewing the client, as a "thou" instead of an "it" is the heart of professional trustworthiness as it makes professionals responsive to their moral accountability to the client. It also makes them more empathetic and caring, which is associated with a wide variety of positive outcomes for clients and patients. The I-Thou relationship cannot, however, be unidirectional. Moral accountability is derived from a second-person standpoint in which persons recognize one another as free and equal members of a moral community. It is only this status that gives them the *authority* to make demands on the other's will.

When clients make moral demands on the professional, they must recognize the mutuality of the second-person, I-Thou, relationship at the heart of moral accountability. Clients must recognize that in providing their service, the professional assumes vulnerability in relation to the client. The relevant vulnerability here is *personal moral vulnerability* in which the professional risks significant personal harm to their moral integrity by potentially being required to perform actions they consider evil. For this reason, the professional can make a *limited* claim on the client to respect that vulnerability. The claim is limited because the vulnerabilities of client/patient and professional are asymmetrical. The professional *chooses* to create his or her vulnerability in taking up a profession that includes legal and legitimate services, some of which he or she happens to find morally objectionable. The individual client or patient is vulnerable because of the monopolization of professional service—an invited monopolization made possible by the promises that professionals will provide reliable service.

Understood this way, the permissibility of conscientious objection can be assessed by explicating the conditions under which a reasonable client or patient should respect the personal moral vulnerability of the professional and accommodate the professional's personal moral objection to a particular practice. For instance, a reasonable client would not accept discriminatory treatment based on the kind of person they happen to be—this is disrespectful to their own status as a free and equal member of the moral community. Nor would a reasonable client or patient accept conscientious objection as a justification of actions that could harm them, either directly or through inaction. Reasonable clients and patients would also reject conscientious objection when it makes access to legal and legitimate services difficult, as this would violate reciprocal justice. Finally, reasonable clients and patients would not accept conscientious objection as a justification to violate the duties of honesty, confidentiality, discretion, respect for autonomy, diligence, loyalty, and beneficence, since these duties are necessary to responsibly care for the client or patient's own vulnerability. For these reasons, a reasonable client is under no obligation to respect conscientious objection from the racist physician or the homophobic social worker.

However, with those limitations in mind, a case can be made for conscientious objection under very limited circumstances, in which a client or patient would lack reasons to reasonably refuse conscientious objection on the part of the professional. Consider the case of an OBGYN who considers late-term abortion to be the killing of an innocent person and, therefore, murder. This view is not grounded in a religious doctrine, but on the view that a late-term fetus possesses the necessary and sufficient properties of a human being. Because late-term abortion is a legal and legitimate service provided by the medical community, his or her objections to the practice are ones rooted in personal morality. Suppose further that when refusing to provide nonemergency late-term abortion service to patients, the OBGYN facilitates a referral to another physician in the same clinic that allows for good continuity of care. Should a reasonable patient respect the OBGYN's moral objections and accept the transfer to the new provider?

This case has several distinctive features to it that make it different from the racist physician or homophobic social worker:

1. Action not Person: the moral objections of the professional are aimed not at the patient as a kind of person, but at the action that is under consideration. When conscientious objection is aimed at the patient as a kind of person, it is an unacceptable breach of the status of the patient as a free and equal member of the moral community. In this case, the OBGYN's objection to late-term abortion is conceptually independent from judgments about the kind of person the patient happens to be.

2. Harm to Patient: the refusal of service in this case is done in a way that provides timely warning and prevention of loss on the part of the patient. The transfer of service is facilitated by the physician and is done seamlessly to ensure continuity of care. Importantly, because the physician has informed the patient in a timely manner, any emotional shock or distress caused by the transfer should be at a minimum.

3. Significant Harm to Professional: in this case the physician believes that late-term abortion is essentially murder. Given this belief, and the direct role the physician would need to play in performing a late-term abortion, a patient, recognizing the professional as a "Thou" should appreciate that any persons of normal psychology would suffer serious moral and emotional harm if forced to perform a procedure they believe is murder.

4. Kind of Reasons: finally, in this case, the reasons offered in support of conscientious objection are by no means idiosyncratic. The physician holds a view that clearly falls into an area of reasonable disagreement within the moral and legal discourse of society. Moreover, the physician's view that a late-term fetus possesses the biological properties sufficient for personhood, are what John Rawls calls "public" reasons.[10] Public reasons are those not anchored in a particular worldview or value system, but are "free standing" in the sense that anyone could hold such reasons independent of their particular comprehensive doctrine. They are reasons that "any reasonable person could reasonably be expected to endorse."[11]

Reasons grounded in a religious tradition, are by contrast, "private" ones, because they are only acceptable to others insofar as they happen to share that tradition. Advocates for conscientious objection often point to religious reasons as the best candidates to justify conscientious objection. However, respect for personhood in a pluralistic society requires that clients and patients are not beholden to the private reasons of professionals, as this would amount to professionals having the right to impose their personal values on those they have promised to serve. The reasons offered by the OBGYN in this case are public in a number of ways, not the least of which is that they are importantly related to the role obligations of the professional. The physician, not unreasonably, believes that the late-term fetus is a person. If this view were correct, and there are strong arguments on both sides of debate about this belief, then the physician's role obligations qua *healer* would forbid performing a late-term abortion (except perhaps in the case where the woman's life was at stake).

Conscientious objection in this case is: (1) done in a way that does not discriminate against the patient; (2) does not harm or significantly inconvenience the patient; (3) is based on public reasons; and (4) involve a practice that would cause significant emotional and moral harm to a person of normal psychology. Given these conditions, a reasonable patient who viewed the physician as a "Thou" and respected the physician's moral and psychological vulnerability should be willing to "release" the physician from the fiduciary obligation to perform the procedure against his or her moral objections. [12]

Some defenders of a stronger right to conscientious objection object to the requirement that, in order to prevent harm to or substantial burden for the patient, professionals exercising conscientious objection must actively arrange a smooth transfer of care to a new provider willing to perform the service in question. This requirement is too strong, they argue, because it demands that the professional facilitate a practice he or she believes is seriously immoral. [13] An OBGYN who believes that late-term abortion is murder, might also believe that actively facilitating the transfer of the patient to a willing provider makes one an accessory to murder.

This view goes too far. By the same logic, the OBGYN would have an obligation to *obstruct* the patient's access to the procedure (perhaps by deceiving the patient into believing the procedure would be illegal), since doing so would prevent a murder from taking place. Indeed, some professionals citing conscientious objection have precisely engaged in such obstruction. A professional community that allowed such obstruction of access to legal and legitimate professional services would not be reliable, and therefore not trustworthy.

A possible compromise might be to forbid professionals from obstructing access to legal and legitimate professional services, but not require them to actively facilitate the transfer of care. The problem with this view is that it fails to adequately respect and care for the invited vulnerability of the client or patient by placing on them the burden of the professional's personal conscience. If, for instance, the OBGYN refuses to actively facilitate the transfer of care, then the burden of "shopping" for a new physician while managing the insurance complications and records transfer falls on the patient. Without active assistance from her current OBGYN, the patient is likely to suffer undue stress and discontinuity of care—both of which are associated with a variety of negative health outcomes. Given that professionals make assurances of their trustworthiness, and create fiduciary relationships with those they serve, allowing such outcomes is unacceptable. Professionals whose conscience would lead them to promote negative outcomes for those they serve in order to satisfy their own sense of moral integrity are not trustworthy.

On the other hand when the professional provides for transfer of care and timely warning, a reasonable patient or client should recognize the professional's own moral vulnerability and accommodate refusal of service based on personal conscience. Refusal of service, whether guided by professional duties, or appropriately limited conscious objection, is an important way in which the professional exercises his or her moral agency. Patients, clients, and employers should recognize the importance of this moral agency and respect its appropriate usage.

WHISTLEBLOWING

Refusal of service is by no means the only time the reasonable client or employer ought to respect the moral agency of the professional. The same moral agency is utilized when professionals engage in whistleblowing. Whistleblowing has become an increasingly common and important practice by which professionals reveal confidential information to expose organizational wrongdoing. In fact, *Time* magazine declared whistleblowers its 2002 "Persons of the Year."

Broadly speaking, whistleblowing can be understood, as Michael Davis defines it, as an activity in which a current or former member of an organization "takes information out of channels to try to stop the organization from doing something that he believes morally wrong."[14] From here a common distinction is made between "internal" and "external" whistleblowing. *Internal whistleblowing* occurs when the professional takes information outside of the authorized channels, but remains within the organization. Typically this means going "over the head" of one's immediate supervisor and disseminating information of wrongdoing to higher levels of management. *External whistleblowing* involves disseminating information of wrongdoing outside the organization, typically to regulatory agencies, law enforcement, or the press.[15]

The need to blow the whistle places the trustworthy professional in a difficult position. On the one hand, to be trustworthy, professionals must commit themselves to the protection of confidential information of their clients, and must develop the virtue of discretion in support of that commitment. Without such a commitment and supporting disposition, professionals would not be worthy of the informational vulnerability that clients must extend to them so they may effectively offer their expert assistance. This is not only true for clients and patients, but for employers as well. Employers must routinely share proprietary information and intimate details of their business affairs with lawyers, accountants, and engineers in order to effectively reap the benefits of expert assistance. For this reason, professionals, both individually and collectively as members of the professional community, invite the trust of clients and employers and promise to be discreet with sensitive organizational information.

However, the duty of confidentiality is not absolute, and neither are the assurances offered to clients and employers. As in refusal of service, trustworthy professionals exercising professional moral agency are responsive to a variety of potentially conflicting duties. Professionals have obligations not only to clients and employers, but also to third parties who are vulnerable to the consequences of their work. Such vulnerability is also an invited one because the professions offer assurances—explicit and implicit promises—to the general public that they will responsibly care for such vulnerability. In making such assurances, professional communities invite the public to trust the reliability of professionals to provide such care.

The ethical dilemma of whistleblowing is created when a professional discovers that his or her client, or employer, is engaging in serious wrongdoing that harms, or threatens to harm, the public. However, the dilemma is more apparent than real. Professionals have an obligation to protect the public, and their fiduciary commitment to confidentiality is clearly limited by their broader duty to the public. The codes of ethics, mission statements, ethics opinions, and other forms of communication used to express the professional's fiduciary commitment make clear that the professional's discretion cannot extend so far as to allow harm to fall on nonconsenting third parties. Even the legal profession, which tends to offer the strongest assurances of confidentiality, allows for a variety of exceptions including disclosures necessary to prevent "reasonably certain death or substantial bodily harm."[16]

While not an ethical dilemma per se, there is nonetheless an important balance that must be achieved here. Revealing confidential information can be very damaging to clients and employers. Because professionals have invited informational trust, they have good reasons to act in ways that minimize the damage created by whistleblowing, provided they can do so in a way that is consistent with their duty to the public.

Even when not strictly bound by confidentiality, discretion requires that professionals, when possible, reveal sensitive information in a manner that minimizes harm. There is actually a surprising amount of agreement in the literature about the general contours of what this proper balance looks like.

Serious Wrongdoing: professionals are obligated to protect the public, and this is the core duty that justifies any form of whistleblowing. For this reason, whistleblowing ought only concern matters in which serious harm to nonconsenting third parties is at stake. Here there is disagreement about the degree and kind of harm required to justify whistleblowing, with De George arguing for a standard of serious bodily harm, while others offer more expansive accounts including serious psychological harm,[17] serious breach of the law,[18] or serious injustices.[19] What these various approaches share, however, is the idea that the wrongdoing involved is of a considerable and serious nature. If any particular harm, no matter how slight, were subject to whistle-blowing, professionals would not be able to secure the informational trust of employers and clients, nor would they be able to offer effective expert assistance.

Reasonable Belief: professionals are not bound by confidentiality if failing to disclose wrongdoing creates serious harm to the public or nonconsenting third parties. However, the professional must have a reasonable belief based on reliable evidence that such harm is actually at stake. Mistaken whistleblowing does happen and, when it does, everyone loses. Organizations suffer a damaged reputation and perhaps the legal costs associated with regulatory investigations; whistleblowers suffer retaliation; and the profession's ability to generate informational trust with employers and clients is compromised.

Priority of Internal Whistleblowing: at the heart of the virtue of discretion is the careful treatment of sensitive information that could injure those who have extended informational trust. For this reason, professionals who have a reasonable belief based on reliable evidence that serious wrongdoing is occurring, or will occur, should, when reasonably efficacious, work internally with their organization to alert key decision makers in an effort to stop or prevent the wrongdoing. Doing so honors the trust the professional secures from both the public and the organization by preventing (or stopping) the wrongdoing while minimizing the damage that the disclosure of information likely causes the organization. Of course, internal disclosure will not always be effective. If the key decision makers within an organization are the perpetrators of the wrongdoing, as in Enron, internal whistleblowing has little reasonable chance of success. Also, in some cases the urgency of the harm may create windows of opportunity too small to allow internal whistleblowing.

External Whistleblowing: when a professional has a reasonable belief based on reliable evidence that serious wrongdoing is, or will be, committed by his or her organization, and internal whistleblowing is not, or is unlikely to be, effective, the professional is justified in taking the relevant information outside the organization. If the professional believes there is a *reasonable chance* that external whistleblowing will stop or prevent the wrongdoing, then he or she is *required* to do so.

Some commentators disagree on this last point, arguing that the retaliation faced by whistleblowers in a context of insufficient legal protections makes external whistleblowing supererogatory and not obligatory.[20] While this view may be appropriate for nonprofessional employees of an organization, it does not go far enough to satisfy that fiduciary commitment that professional communities make to safeguard the public welfare. Public trust would hardly be secured by professional communities that were committed to protecting the public only when it was easy for them to do so.

"AVOIDING" WHISTLEBLOWING

Because professionals have an obligation to exercise professional moral agency, reasonable employers and clients should recognize the genuine ethical limits to any professional's fiduciary commitment to confidentiality. While clients and employers are informationally vulnerable to the professionals who serve them, professionals are morally vulnerable to their clients and employers insofar as clients and employers have the power to threaten potential whistleblowers and retaliate against actual ones. In accepting the professional's offer of expert assistance, clients and employers invite the professional's trust that they will not abuse the professional's moral vulnerability. Clients or employers should, therefore, respect the professional's moral agency and protect sincere whistleblowers from formal or informal whistleblowing. Moreover, organizations generally have good reasons to, as Davis puts it, *prevent* whistleblowing by creating channels of communication and an organizational culture that promotes the authorized disclosure of wrongdoing.[21]

Whistleblowing involves going outside approved channels of organizational communication in order to expose serious wrongdoing. Given the damage that comes from external whistleblowing, employers have good reason to prevent it, not in sense of suppressing the disclosure of wrongdoing, but by encouraging and authorizing such disclosures internally, effectively making them a normal part of the organization. Doing so requires the creation of a just, transparent, and responsive communicative organizational culture. An organization has a just communicative culture when: (1) communication and decision-making procedures emphasize transparency, reciprocity, and the invitation for dissent; (2) there are guaranteed communicative rights for organizational members that protect them within the organization's communicative procedures; and (3) dispositions on the part of management to be genuinely responsive to member feedback are present and encouraged by the organization.

With a reasonably just communicative culture in place, employers encourage the internal disclosure of wrongdoing, which allows the organization to take corrective action without the variety of harms created by external whistleblowing. There is good reason to believe that whistleblowers would respond positively to such a culture. The stereotype (among management) that whistleblowers are disloyal opportunists is not borne out by the facts. The vast majority of external whistleblowers (84 percent) go outside their organization only *after* disclosing the wrongdoing internally.[22] If organizations created inclusive and transparent decision-making procedures and "lattice-like"[23] pathways of communication that encouraged and authorized disclosure of wrongdoing to a variety of levels of the organization, whistle-blowing—understood as taking information outside of approved channels of communication—would likely become quite rare.

A just communicative organizational culture not only better respects professional moral agency but provides a variety of "bottom line" benefits to the organization itself. As *The Economist* notes "[b]ad news tends to come out eventually, and looks worse if it appears that bosses tried to suppress it."[24] When organizations suppress such disclosures they increase the chances of external whistleblowing and the organizational damage that such whistle-blowing often creates. More importantly, an unjust communicative culture promotes epistemically and morally impoverished decision-making procedures, which increases the chances the organization will make poor decisions or engage in wrongdoing. Perhaps the most famous example of this is the Challenger disaster in which management at Morton Thiokol unilaterally authorized the launch over the objections of the engineering staff. A more inclusive decision-making procedure would have prevented an accident that took seven lives and cost billions of dollars. The incident turned out to be all the more damaging to NASA and Morton Thiokol when efforts to conceal the true nature of the incident led engineer Roger Boisjoly to disclose to government investigators how the flawed decision-making process led to the irresponsible decision to launch.

The benefits of organizational communicative justice go far beyond the issue of whistleblowing. Organizational justice generates employee trust, which is positively associated with employee loyalty, performance, job satisfaction, and lower turnover rates.[25] Tom Tyler argues that this can be attributed to the role that fair treatment plays in the relational identity of agents within groups. Agents consider fair treatment and respect as indicators of their worth to the organization. When treated unfairly or with disrespect, organizational members perceive themselves to be unvalued by the organization, and because of the importance of self-esteem in one's identity, are likely to disassociate their well-being from the organization's. Perceived trustworthiness, on the other hand, works hand in hand with employee self-identification. As a matter of self-esteem, when individuals are treated fairly and with respect, individuals are much more likely to integrate the organization and its well-being as an important component of their existential self-understanding. When such "group identification" occurs, employees will naturally be more loyal and diligent because they have integrated their sense of well-being with that of the organization. The result is the acquisition of social capital, which employers can use to create loyalty and diligence without relying on external constraints such as incentive, or disciplinary programs, which tend to be "cumbersome and ineffective."[26]

Clients and employers have good reasons to create a communicative culture that encourages the disclosure of bad news. Morally, such a culture promotes the prevention of wrongdoing. It also promotes respect for the moral agency of the professional. This respect in turn leads to increased loyalty and better job performance from professionals who judge their organization to be trustworthy. Finally, there are real epistemic gains to be made through a just communicative organizational culture. "Echo chambers" are discouraged, while the expert resources of the organization are more fluidly combined in decision-making processes that are transparent, symmetrical, and open.

CONCLUSION

The invitation professionals make to clients, patients, employers, and the general public is neither global nor absolute. Because trust is "three-part," the professional's invitation to trust is relativized to the appropriate promotion of the profession's telos, and is limited by the professional's obligations to third parties. Professionals, therefore, should not be trustworthy in every respect and in light of every extension of trust. When clients, patients, or employers make requests that are inappropriate, professionals should exercise their professional moral agency and refuse such requests.

Likewise, professionals are justified, indeed obligated, to disclose serious wrongdoings committed by clients or employers, despite their invitation to informational trust. The assurances of confidentiality made by professionals are not absolute, but must be understood in light of the other duties that professionals must satisfy. Rather than attempt to suppress the disclosure of such wrongdoings, organizations are better served by creating an open communicative culture in which such disclosures are routine.

NOTES

1. Paul Faber, "Client and Professional" in *Ethics for the Professions*, ed. John Rowan and Samuel Zinaich, Jr. (Belmont, CA: Wadsworth, 2003), 128.

2. E.C. Hui, "Doctors as Fiduciaries: A Legal Construct of the Patient-Physician Relationship," *Hong Kong Journal of Medicine* 11, no. 6 (2005): 527–29.

3. Edmund Pellegrino and David Thomasma, *The Virtues of Medical Practice,* 31–50.

4. Edmund Pellegrino, "The Physician's Conscience, Conscience Clauses, and Religious Belief: A Catholic Perspective," *Fordham Urban Law Journal* 30, no. 1 (2002): 220–44.

5. Pellegrino, "The Physician's Conscience, Conscience Clauses, and Religious Belief: A Catholic Perspective," 228.

6. Mark Wicclair,"Conscientious Objection in Medicine," *Bioethics* 14, no. 3 (2000): 205–23.

7. Julian Savalescu, "Ethics: Conscientious Objection in Medicine," *BMJ The British Medical Journal* 332, no. 7536 (2006): 294–97.

8. Wicclair, "Pharmacies, Pharmacists, and Conscientious Objection," *Kennedy Institute of Ethics Journal* 16, no. 3 (2006): 232.

9. Julian Savulescu, "Conscientious Objection in Medicine," 297.

10. John Rawls, *Political Liberalism* (New York: Columbia University Press: 1996), 212–47.

11. John Rawls, *Political Liberalism.*

12. See, Julie Cantor and Ken Baum, "The Limits of Conscientious Objection—May Pharmacists Refuse to Fill Prescriptions for Emergency Contraception?" *New England Journal of Medicine* 351, no. 19 (2004): 2008–12.

13. R. Alta Chara, "The Celestial Fire of Conscience—Refusing to Deliver Medical Care," New *England Journal of Medicine* 352 (2005): 2471–73.

14. Michael Davis, "Avoiding the Tragedy of Whistleblowing," *Business and Professional Ethics Journal* 8, no. 4 (1989): 5.

15. Richard de George, *Business Ethics* (New York: Prentice Hall, 2010), 298–318.

16. American Bar Association, *Model Rules for Professional Conduct,* http://www.americanbar.org/groups/professional_responsibility/publications/model_rules_of _professional_conduct/rule_1_6_confidentiality_of_information.html

17. Gene James, "Whistleblowing: Its Moral Justifications," in *Business Ethics: Readings and Cases in Corporate Morality,* ed. W. Michael Hoffman and Robert Frederick and Mark Schwartz (New York: McGraw Hill, 1990): 291–302.

18. W. Michael Hoffman and Mark Schwartz, "The Morality of Whistleblowing: A Commentary on Richard De George," *Journal of Business Ethics* 157 (2015): 787.

19. Velasquez, *Business Ethics* (Upper Saddle River, NJ: Prentice Hall/Pearson, 1990).

20. Mike Martin, "Whistleblowing: Professionalism, Personal Life, and Shared Responsibility for Safety in Engineering," *Business and Professional Ethics Journal* 11, no. 2 (1992): 28.

21. Davis, "Avoiding the Tragedy of Whistleblowing," 10.

22. Ethics Resource Center, *Inside the Mind of a Whistleblower* (2012): http://erc.webair.com/? q=resource/inside-mind-whistleblower12

23. Davis, "Avoiding the Tragedy of Whistleblowing," 12.

24. *The Economist,* "The Age of the Whistleblower," December 5, 2015. http://www.economist.com/news/business/21679455-life-getting-better-those-who-expose-wrongdoing-companies-continue-fight

25. Tom Tyler, "Trust Within Organizations," *Personnel Review* 32, no. 5 (2003): 556–68.

26. Tom Tyler, "Why Do People Rely on Others? Social Identity and Social Aspects of Trust," in *Trust in Society,* 285–307.

Conclusion

Professionals have good reasons to invite, develop, and honor the trust of clients, patients, and the general public. Such trust promotes effective professional practice, the flourishing of professionals, and honors the obligations professionals have to those they serve. Because the establishment and development of trust requires successfully communicating one's trustworthiness to trust-evaluators, professionals have good reasons to be effectively trustworthy through the communal establishment of a robust reputation for professional roles, and through interpersonal signaling and impression management.

Given the importance of trust and effective trustworthiness in professional practice, a trust-based approach to professional ethics supports a number of important conclusions about ethics education, the evaluation of professional conduct, the role of promising in professional ethics, and the importance of professional moral agency.

PROFESSIONAL IDENTITY AND CHARACTER EDUCATION

For some time, professional ethics, as practiced in the professions, has drifted toward a *compliance paradigm* in which professional responsibility consists of observing rules, such as ethics codes, backed by disciplinary systems. Viewing professional ethics this way is insufficient to protect those who are served by professions and to develop the kind of robust trust necessary for effective professional practice. The compliance paradigm is essentially a "hedge" that disincentivizes misconduct rather than incentivizes the responsible care of those who depend on professionals. It also encourages "loophole" and "checklist" mentalities in which ethics comes to be seen an obstacle, rather than a foundation for professional flourishing and responsibility.

All too often, in this paradigm, professional ethics "education" consists of an isolated course that reviews the ethics code and the profession's disciplinary regime. The blameworthiness of professional misconduct becomes relativized to conduct for which one will be punished.

While compliance certainly has its place in professional ethics, the responsible care of the interests entrusted to professionals is better secured through the development of dispositional trustworthiness. Dispositionally trustworthy professionals possess character virtues that make them *internally* reliable to responsibly care for the client or patient's vulnerabilities because such professionals are positively motivated to engage in ethical conduct.

The development of the professional virtues requires the work of the profession as an ethical community to establish education and training programs that promote a *culture of trustworthiness*. In this *authenticity paradigm*, the professional virtues are linked with one's sense of self-identity as a professional. When successful, professionals responsibly care for clients and patients because *it is who they are* as professionals.

In educational settings, giving the professional virtues practical credibility requires a decentered approach to ethics training. Formal courses in professional ethics are important because virtues are not simply habits, but are principled dispositions linking of motivation with moral insight. However, ethics courses cannot exist as stand-alone entities, cut off from the broader practice and culture of professional education. Leaders of professional training programs should strive to create an ethical culture by which the professional virtues are studied and *practiced* in a variety of instructional contexts. These might include mentorship programs, internship with ethical requirements, and ethics training decentered through the professional curriculum. By decentering ethics training, professional virtues gain practical credibility for students because the themes of their formal ethics education are reiterated throughout the professional curriculum. When a would-be professional studies the underlying principles of professional ethics, and then experiences those principles in their practical courses, internships and mentor programs, the professional virtues become more than philosophical ideas, but a part of the common sense of everyday practice.

Professional communities must also advocate for working conditions that promote the professional virtues. For instance, chronic overwork and high stress leads to *emotional exhaustion* in many professionals. Such professionals *depersonalize* clients and patients, making it harder for them to care for their clients and patients. Professional education programs have good reason to focus on resilience as an important virtue and provide training to assist professionals in managing work stress in ways that promote professional responsibility. Professional communities should also advocate for reforms in these kinds of working conditions. Organizations that employ professionals also have good reasons to avoid the conditions that create emotional exhaustion. Emotionally exhausted professionals are less productive, more likely to create dissatisfaction with clients, and more likely to leave their job. Improving job performance and reducing turnover are good "bottom line" reasons to promote the kinds of working conditions in which professionals can serve their clients and patients *well.*

Compliance still needs to play an important role in professional ethics. Compliance systems highlight the importance the professional community gives to proper care of clients and patients, protect clients and patients from those lacking good character, or from those who occasionally need a "nudge" to do the right thing. However, compliance cannot replace the development of dispositional trustworthiness.

THE IMPORTANCE OF APPEARANCES

In order to invite and develop trust with clients, patient, and the general public, professionals must not only be trustworthy, they must be able to effectively communicate that trustworthiness. When *effectively trustworthy,* professionals are able to utilize the reputation of their social role to establish prima facie trust, and then use their impression management to signal their interpersonal trustworthiness.

The importance of effective trustworthiness supports the idea that *appearances matter* in professional ethics. This is most clear in the case of conflicts of interest. Many professionals think conflicts of interest exist only when a personal interest undermines their professional judgment. Mere appearances of such conflicts are in no way blameworthy, but are simply "red flags" that bear close scrutiny. This view is mistaken because it fails to appreciate the ways in which "potential" conflicts create real threats to the trustworthiness of the professional— threats that are often unintentional and unconscious. Moreover, it underestimates the importance of appearances in developing trust with clients and the public. Because professionals have good reasons, including a moral obligation, to develop trust with clients, patients, and the general public, they ought not act in ways that undermine that trust. Conflicts of interest, therefore, are better understood as arrangements by which a reasonable observer (e.g., a client or member of the public) would conclude that a normal professional would be tempted to prioritize secondary interests over his or her professional responsibilities. This view better protects those reliant on professionals and signals to trust evaluators the importance the professional gives to his or her trustworthiness. The view that even an avoidable appearance of impropriety is enough to create a blameworthy arrangement is already common in some areas of law, such as judicial ethics, and is gaining increasing acceptance in other fields such as medicine and engineering.

THE MORAL LIMITS OF PROFESSIONAL TRUSTWORTHINESS

A possible objection to a trust-based professional ethics is that professionals should not be worthy of all forms of trust. Patients, clients, and employers sometimes trust professionals to act in ways that violate their professional obligations, and such trust should not be honored.

When professionals invite trust, and signal their trustworthiness, they by no means invite global trust, but three-part trust. The invitation to trust is limited to the responsible care of the appropriate interests entrusted to the professional in light of the telos of the profession and the obligations the professional owes to others. For this reason, professionals should decline to honor trust that is inappropriate. For instance, a patient might trust a physician to feed his or her opioid habit, but honoring such trust is inappropriate—indeed prohibited, given the physician's promise to "do no harm" and to promote the public health.

Likewise, a client or employer might trust an engineer to keep secret serious wrongdoing by his or her organization. While engineers invite informational trust, that invitation is neither global nor absolute, but must be understood in light of the telos of engineering and the assurances the engineer has made to peers and the general public. When the wrongdoing poses a serious threat to public safety, and the engineer has tried to resolve the issue internally, the invitation for informational trust does not preclude justified external whistleblowing. The engineer's invitation to informational trust does, however, provide support for a measured approach to whistleblowing by which the engineer acts on reasonable evidence, favors internal over external whistleblowing, and discloses information in a way that does not unnecessarily harm the organization or its members.

PROMISES IN PROFESSIONAL ETHICS

This book began with a consideration of the criticisms of the "promising approach" to professional ethics. Critics contend that grounding professional role obligations on promising was, at least, an incomplete approach because it could not explain why professionals should make certain promises to clients, patients, and the general public. Critics also contend that the commitments made by professionals are too implicit to be well understood as promises.

While critics are right that professional role obligations cannot be understood in terms of promising *alone*, promises still play an important role in professional ethics. Understood as assurances of one's trustworthiness, explicit and implicit promising plays an important role in trust development. The specific promises made by professionals are oriented by the reasons for inviting trust in light of the professional telos. Given the vulnerabilities created by reliance on professionals, professionals need to invite trust and signal their trustworthiness through a variety of assurances that they can be relied upon to honor the trust extended to them. These assurances are invitations to trust and can be reasonably understood as promises. Some of these promises are explicit, as in oaths, while others are implied, created by the totality of the circumstances at play when someone presents him or herself as a bona fide *professional*.

These promises are important because once made, they create clear and nonnegotiable commitment to responsible ethical conduct. Thus regardless of the reasons why professionals take oaths and present themselves as professionals, when they do so, they must recognize that, at the very least, they have *promised* to responsibly care for the appropriate interests entrusted to them—an obligation they can be released from only with the consent of those who have accepted their promise and placed their well-being in the professional's hands.

The content of these implied promises comes from the reputation of the profession and communicative gestures such as oaths and the promulgation of codes of ethics. This shows that professional ethics relies on the work of professions as robust ethical communities. One could understand these commitments as the community's settled judgment as to the kind of conduct necessary to promote professional trustworthiness. While revisable, they represent the community's reasoned view on what is required—and what must be promised— to be a trustworthy professional.

A REALISTIC UTOPIANISM

The demands of trust-based professional ethics are high, but they should not be unfamiliar. It is generally recognized that trust is at the heart of professional practice. Moreover, the professions engage, however imperfectly, in many of the recommendations advanced by trust-based professional ethics. Nursing and education already take seriously the development of trustworthy dispositions in the educational process. Engineering ethics has also been moving toward virtue-based approaches to ethics education and training. The legal profession has long recognized that appearances of impropriety are inconsistent with the trust extended to judges. The medical profession has championed the idea of its professional practice as a "moral enterprise." Finally, the engineering profession is well known for resisting the idea that the professional is a mere agent to the client. Most engineering ethics codes make clear that the first duty of engineers is to protect the public.

The different professional communities serve as exemplars by which a variety of best practices can be reconstructed into a coherent ideal for the professions generally. The professions have good reasons to develop the professional virtues in practitioners; to recognize the importance of the appearances created by professional conduct; to see professional practice as a moral enterprise; and to exercise professional moral agency while responsibly serving clients, patients, and employers.

Grounded as it is in the actual practices of the various professions, trust-based professional ethics takes a "realistically utopian" view of professional ethics. Such a utopianism is but an idealized reflection of current professional practices and offers a path for the professions to become more fully what they are. Such utopianism is also realistic in the sense that professionals have a variety of good reasons, not just moral obligations, to develop effective trustworthiness in concert with their broader ethical communities. Professionals have a moral obligation to do so, but they have good instrumental and ethical reasons as well. Developing trust with patients and clients through effective trustworthiness promotes the flourishing of professionals, the "existential joy" of professional practice, and the bottom line of professional enterprises. Effective trustworthiness also buttresses the public trust necessary for professional communities to continue to enjoy their prestige and relatively self-governing status.

Becoming effectively trustworthy is not easy, and it requires the work of a healthy ethical community, but professionals who value the telos of their profession will see in effective trustworthiness a reflection of their own aspirations—to be worthy of the trust they invite from their clients, patients, students, employers, and the public at large.

Bibliography

Adams, Robert. *A Theory of Virtue*. Oxford, UK: Oxford University Press, 2006.

Alexandra, Andrew and Miller, Seamus. "Ethical Theory, "Common Morality," and Professional Obligations." *Theoretical Medicine and Bioethics* 30 (2009): 69–80.

————. *Ethics in Practice: Moral Theory and the Professions*. New South Wales, AUS: University of New South Wales Press, 2009.

————. "Needs, Moral Self-Consciousness, and Professional Roles." *Professional Ethics* 5, no. 1 (1996): 43–61.

Andre, Judith. "Role Morality as a Complex Instance of Ordinary Morality." *American Philosophical Quarterly* 28, no.1 (1991): 73–80.

Bacharach, Michael and Diego Gambetta. "Trust in Signs." In *Trust and Society*, ed. Karen Cook, 148–84. New York: Russell Sage Foundation, 2001.

Bayles, Michael. *Professional Ethics*, 2nd ed. Belmont, CA: Wadsworth, 1989.

Baier, Annette. "Trust and Antitrust." *Ethics* 96, no. 2 (1986): 231–60.

————. "Trust and its Vulnerabilities." In *The Tanner Lectures on Human Values*, Vol. 13. Salt Lake City: University of Utah Press, 1992.

Banaji, Mahzarin and Anthony Greenwald. *Blindspot: Hidden Biases of Good People*. New York: Delacorte Press, 2013.

Batson, C. Daniel, Pamela Cochran, Marshall Beiderman, James Blosser, Maurice Ryan and Bruce Vogt. "Failure to Help When in a Hurry: Callousness or Conflict?" *Personality and Social Psychology Bulletin* 4, no. 1 (1978): 97–101.

Braus, Edie. "Common Misconceptions About Professional Licensure." *American Journal of Nursing* 112, no. 10 (2012): 55–59.

Brien, Andrew. "Professional Ethics and the Culture of Trust." *Journal of Business Ethics* 17, no. 4 (1998): 391–409.

Brody, Howard. "Clarifying Conflict of Interest." *The American Journal of Bioethics* 11, no. 1 (2011): 23–28.

————. "Medical Organizations and Commercial Conflicts of Interest: Ethical Issues." *Annals of Family Medicine* 8 (2010): 354–58.

Cantor, Julie, and Ken Baum. "The Limits of Conscientious Objection—May Pharmacists Refuse to Fill Prescriptions for Emergency Contraception?" *New England Journal of Medicine* 351, no. 19 (2004): 2008–12.

Chara, R. Alta "The Celestial Fire of Conscience—Refusing to Deliver Medical Care." *New England Journal of Medicine* 352 (2005): 2471–73.

Chriss, James. "Habermas, Goffman, and Communicative Action: Implications for Professional Practice." *American Sociological Review* 60 (1995): 545–65.

Cohen, Marc and John Dienhart. "Moral and Amoral Conceptions of Trust, with an Application in Organizational Ethics." *Journal of Business Ethics* 112 (2013): 1–13.

Cox, Damien, Marguerite LaCaze, and Michael Levine, "Should We Strive for Integrity?" *Journal of Value Inquiry* 33 (1999): 519–30.

Crigger, Nancy and Nelda Godfrey. "From the Inside Out: A New Approach to Teaching Professional Identity Formation and Professional Ethics." *Journal of Professional Nursing* 30, no. 5 (2014): 376–82.

D'Cruz, Jason. "Trust, Trustworthiness, and the Moral Consequence of Consistency." *Journal of the American Philosophical Association* 1, no. 3 (2015): 476–84.

Dana, Jason and George Lowenstein. "A Social Science Perspective on Gifts to Physicians from Industry." *Journal of the American Medical Association* 290, no. 2 (2003): 252–55.

Darley, John, C. Daniel Batson, "From Jerusalem to Jericho: A Study of Situational and Dispositional Variables in Helping Behavior." *Journal of Personality and Social Psychology* 27, no. 1 (1973): 100–108.

Darwall, Stephan. *The Second-Person Standpoint: Morality, Respect and Accountability.* Cambridge, MA: Harvard University Press, 2006.

Davis, Michael. "Thinking Like an Engineer: The Place of a Code of Ethics in the Practice of a Profession." *Philosophy and Public Affairs* 20, no. 2 (1991): 150–67.

――――. "Avoiding the Tragedy of Whistleblowing." *Business and Professional Ethics Journal* 8, no. 4 (1989): 3–19.

de George, Richard. *Business Ethics*. New York: Prentice Hall, 2010.

Dienhart, John. "Rationality, Ethical Codes, and an Egalitarian Justification of Ethical Expertise: Implications for Professions and Organizations." *Business Ethics Quarterly* 5, no. 3 (1995): 419–50.

Dobson, John. "Monkey Business: A Neo-Darwinist Approach to Ethics Codes." *Financial Analysts Journal* 61, no. 3 (2005): 59–64.

Dorris, John. *Lack of Character: Personality and Moral Behavior*. New York: Cambridge University Press, 2002.

Dostoevsky, Fyodor. *The Brothers Karamazov*. Translated by David Magarshack. London: Penguin, 1982.

Elster, Jon. *Sour Grapes*. Cambridge, MA: Cambridge University Press, 1983.

Epstein, Elizabeth and Laura Delgado. "Understanding and Addressing Moral Distress." *Online Journal of Issues in Nursing* 15, no. 3 (2010): Manuscript 1.

Erde, Edmund "Conflicts of Interest in Medicine: A Philosophical and Ethical Morphology," in *Conflicts of Interest in Clinical Practice and Research*, ed. Roy Speece, David Shim and Allen Buchanan (New York: Oxford University Press, 1996), 12–41.

Ethics Resource Center, *Inside the Mind of a Whistleblower* (2012): http://erc.webair.com/?q=resource/inside-mind-whistleblower12.

Faber, Paul. "Client and Professional." In *Ethics for the Professions*, ed. John Rowan and Samuel Zinaich, Jr., 125–34. Belmont, CA: Wadsworth, 2003.

Fallowfield, L.J., V.A. Jenkins, and H.A. Beveridge. "Truth May Hurt, but Deceit Hurts More: Communication in Palliative Care." *Palliative Medicine* 16 (2002): 297–303.

Florman, Samuel C. *The Existential Pleasures of Engineering*. New York: St. Martin's Griffin, 1994.

Freedman, Benjamin. "A Meta-ethics for Professional Morality." *Ethics* 89, no. 1 (1978): 1–19.

Garfinkel, Harold. "A Conception of, and Experiments with 'Trust' as a Condition of Stable Concerted Action." In *Motivation and Social Interaction*, ed. O.J. Harvey. New York: The Ronald Press, 1963.

――――. "Studies in the Routine Grounds of Everyday Activities." In *Studies in Ethnomethodology*. Englewood Cliffs, NJ: Prentice Hall, 1967.

Gert, Bernard and Charles Culver. *Bioethics: A Systematic Approach*. Oxford, UK: Oxford University Press, 2006.

Gewirth, Alan. "Professional Ethics: The Separatist Thesis." *Ethics* 96, no. 2 (1986): 282–300.

Goffman, Erving. *The Presentation of the Self in Everyday Life*. New York: Doubleday, 1959.

Goodin, Robert. *Protecting the Vulnerable*. Chicago: University of Chicago Press, 1985.

Grady, Christine, Marion Davis, Karen Soeken, Patricia O'Donnell, Carol Taylor, Adrienne Farrar and Connie Ulrich. "Does Nursing Education Influence the Moral Action of Practicing Nurses and Social Workers?" *American Journal of Biomedical Ethics* 8, no. 4 (2008): 4–11.

Graham, David, David Campen, Rita Hui, Michele Spence, Craig Cheetham, Gerald Levy, Stanford Shoor, Wayne Ray. "Risk of Acute Myocardial Infarction and Sudden Cardiac Death in Patients Treated with Cyclo-Oxygenase 2 Selective and Non-Selective Non-Steroidal Anti-Inflammatory Drugs: Nested Case Control Study." *Lancet* 365, no. 9458 (2005): 475–81.

Gunther, Klaus. *The Sense of Appropriateness*. New York: SUNY Press, 1993.

Habermas, Jürgen. *Between Facts and Norms*. Translated by William Regh. Cambridge, MA: MIT Press, 1998.

————. "On the Employment of Practical Reason," in *Justification and Application*. Translated by Ciaran Cronen. Cambridge, MA: MIT Press, 1993.

————. *Theory of Communicative Action*, Vol. 1. Translated by Thomas McCarthy. Boston: Beacon Press, 1984.

————. *The Theory of Communicative Action*, Vol. 2. Translated by Thomas McCarthy. Boston: Beacon Press, 1987.

Hall, Mark, Elizabeth Dugan, Beiyao Zheng, and Aneil Mishra. "Trust in Physicians and Medical Institutions: What Is It? Can It Be Measured? and Does It Matter? *Milbank Quarterly* 79, no. 4 (2001): 613–39.

Hardin, Russell. "Conceptions and Explanations of Trust." In *Trust in Society*, edited by Karen Cook, 3–39. New York: Russell Sage Foundation, 2001.

————. "The Street-Level Epistemology of Trust." *Politics and Society* 21 (1993): 505–29.

————. *Trust and Trustworthiness*. New York: Russell Sage Foundation, 2002.

————. "Trustworthiness" *Ethics* 107, no. 1 (1996): 26–42.

Harman, Gilbert. "The Non-existence of Character Traits." *Proceedings of the Aristotelian Society* 100, 223–26.

Hart, H.L.A. "Are There any Natural Rights?" *Philosophical Review* 64, no. 2 (1955): 175–91.

Heim, Linda. "Identifying and Addressing Potential Conflict of Interest: A Professional Medical Organization's Code of Ethics." *Annals of Family Medicine* 8, no. 4 (2010): 359–61.

Hoffman W. Michael and Mark Schwartz. "The Morality of Whistleblowing: A Commentary on Richard De George." *Journal of Business Ethics* 157 (2015): 771–81.

Hui, E.C. "Doctors as Fiduciaries: A Legal Construct of the Patient-Physician Relationship." *Hong Kong Journal of Medicine* 11, no. 6 (2005): 527–29.

Hume, David. *A Treatise on Human Nature*. Oxford, UK: Clarendon Press, 1967.

Hursthouse, Rosalind. "Virtue Theory." *Stanford Encyclopedia of Philosophy*, ed. Edward Zalta. http://plato.stanford.edu/entries/ethics-virtue/, last accessed May 10, 2016.

Institute of Medicine, "Conflict of Interest and Development of Clinical Practice Guidelines." In *Conflict of Interest in Medical Research, Education, and Practice*. Washington, DC: National Academies Press; 2009:189–215.

James, Gene. "Whistleblowing: Its Moral Justifications." In *Business Ethics: Readings and Cases in Corporate Morality*, ed. W. Michael Hoffman and Robert Frederick and Mark Schwartz. New York: McGraw Hill, 1990: 291–302.

Jameton, Andrew. "Dilemmas of Moral Distress: Moral Responsibility and Nursing Practice." *AWHONNS Clinical Issues in Perinatal & Women's Health Nursing* 4, no. 4 (1993): 542–51.

Jones, Karen. "Trustworthiness." *Ethics* 123, no. 1 (2012): 61–85.

Kuhse, Helga. *Caring: Nurses, Women and Ethics*. New York: Wiley-Blackwell, 1997.

Locke, John. *Two Treatises of Civil Government*. New York: Cambridge University Press, 1988.

Luebke, Neil. "Conflict of Interest as a Moral Category." *Business & Professional Ethics Journal* 6 (1987): 66–81.

Luhmann, Niklas. *Trust and Power*. Chichester: John Wiley & Sons, 1979.

MacIntyre, Alasdair. *After Virtue*. South Bend, IN: Notre Dame University Press, 1981.

Martin, Mike and Roland Schinzinger. *Ethics in Engineering,* 4th ed. Boston: McGraw Hill, 2005.

McCann, Clare, Elizabeth Beddoe, Katie McCormick, Peter Huggard, Sally Kedge, Carole Adamson, and Jayne Huggard. "Resilience in the Health Professions: A Review of Recent Literature." *International Journal of Wellbeing* 3, no. 1 (2013): 60–81.

Mill, John Stuart. *Utilitarianism.* New York: Hackett Publishing, 2002.

Nickel, Phillip. "Trust and Obligation-Ascription." *Ethical Theory and Moral Practice* 10 (2007): 309–19.

Newton, Lisa. "In Defense of the Traditional Nurse," *Nursing Outlook* 29, no. 6 (1981): 348–54.

Pellegrino, Edmund "The Medical Profession as a Moral Community." *Bulletin of the New York Academy of Medicine* 66, no. 3 (1990): 221–32.

———. "The Physician's Conscience, Conscience Clauses, and Religious Belief: A Catholic Perspective." *Fordham Urban Law Journal* 30, no. 1 (2002): 220–44.

Pellegrino, Edmund and David Thomasma. *The Virtues in Medical Practice.* New York: Oxford University Press, 1993.

People v. Pautler, 47 P.3d 1175, 1184 (Colo. 2002).

Presley, Holly. "Vioxx and the Merck Team Effort." *The Kenan Institute for Ethics at Duke University* (2009): https://web.duke.edu/kenanethics/CaseStudies/Vioxx.pdf.

Rachels, James. "Why Privacy Is Important." *Philosophy and Public Affairs* 4, no. 4 (1975): 323–33.

Rawls, John. *A Theory of Justice: Revised Edition.* Cambridge, MA: Belknap Press, 1999.

———. *Political Liberalism.* New York: Columbia University Press: 1996.

Rothman, David, Walter McDonald, Carol Berkowitz, Susan Chimonas, Catherine DeAngeles, Ralph Hale, Steven Nissen, June Osborne, James Scully, Gerald Thomson, and David Wofsy. "Professional Medical Associations and Their Relation to Industry." *Journal of the American Medical Association* 301, no. 13 (2009): 1367–72.

Savalescu, Julian. "Ethics: Conscientious Objection in Medicine." *BMJ The British Medical Journal* 332, no. 7536 (2006): 294–97.

Scanlon, Thomas. "Promises and Practices." *Philosophy and Public Affairs,* 19 no. 3 (1990): 199–226.

Sellman, Derek. "On Being of Good Character: Nurse Education and the Assessment of Good Character." *Nurse Education Today* 27 (2007): 762–67.

Sidgwick, Henry. *The Methods of Ethics.* London: MacMillan, 1907.

Simpson, Timothy. "Trustworthiness and Moral Character." *Ethical Theory and Moral Practice* 16 (2013): 543–57.

Smith, John-Christian. "Strong Separatism in Professional Ethics." *Professional Ethics,* 3 (1994): 117–40.

Sousa, Sharon, Ruth Griffin, and Barbara Krainovich-Miller. "Professional Nursing Competence and Good Moral Character: A Policy Exemplar." *Journal of Nursing Law* 15, no. 2 (2012): 51–60.

Southwood, Nicholas and David Friedrich. "Promises Beyond Assurance." *Philosophical Studies* 144 (2009): 261–80.

Sreenivasan, Gopol. "Errors about Errors: Virtue Theory and Trait Attribution." *Mind* 111, no. 441 (2002): 47–68.

Sussman, Jeff. "Do Things Really Go Better with Coke?" *Journal of Family Practice* 58, no. 12 (2009): 630.

Tyler, Tom. "Trust Within Organizations." *Personnel Review* 32, no. 5 (2003): 556–68.

———. "Why Do People Rely on Others? Social Identity and Social Aspects of Trust." In *Trust in Society,* ed. Karen Cook, 285–307. New York: Russell Sage Foundation, 2001.

United States Courts. *Code of Conduct for United States Judges.* http://www.uscourts.gov/judges-judgeships/code-conduct-united-states-judges#d, last accessed May 10, 2016.

Valasquez, Manuel. *Business Ethics.* Upper Saddle River, NJ: Prentice Hall/Pearson, 1990.

Veatch, Robert. "Is Trust in Professionals a Coherent Concept?" In *Ethics, Trust and the Professions,* ed. Edmund Pellegrino, Robert Veatch and John Langan, 159–76. Washington, DC: Georgetown University Press: 1991.

Weber, Max. *Economy and Society*. Edited and Translated by G. Roth and C. Wittich. Los Angeles: University of California Press, 1968.

Wells, John. "Efficient Office Space for a Successful Practice." *Family Practice Management Journal* 14, no. 5, 2007: 46–50.

Wicclair, Mark. "Conscientious Objection in Medicine." *Bioethics* 14, no. 3 (2000): 205–23.

————. "Pharmacies, Pharmacists, and Conscientious Objection." *Kennedy Institute of Ethics Journal* 13, no. 3 (2006): 225–50.

Williams, Bernard. "Internal and External Reasons." In *Rational Action*, ed. Ross Harrison, 101–13. Cambridge, MA: Cambridge University Press, 1979.

————. "Utilitarianism and Self-Indulgence." In *Moral Luck: Philosophical Papers: 1973–1980*. Cambridge: Cambridge University Press, 1981: 40–53.

Winslow, Gerald. "From Loyalty to Advocacy: A New Metaphor for Nursing." *Hastings Center Report* 14, no. 3 (1984): 32–40.

Index

About the Author

Terrence M. Kelly is assistant professor at the University of Alaska Anchorage where he works in the Philosophy Department and the Alaska Ethics Center. Previous works include: "Conflicts About Conflicts of Interest"; "Unlocking the Iron Cage: Public Administration in the Democratic Theory of Jürgen Habermas"; "Sociological not Political: Rawls and the Reconstructive Social Sciences"; and "New Public Management and the Demise of Popular Sovereignty" (with Mary Timney); and other articles.

He is also chairperson of the Anchorage Municipal Board of Ethics and provides ethics workshops to a variety of professional communities in Alaska. An avid skier, cyclist, musician, and angler, he lives in Anchorage, Alaska with his wife, Cheryl, and his son, Elias.